SCHERER SCHNEIDER **PAULICK**

Oi Partners Inc
www.sspcorp.net

One North Franklin Street
Suite 1100
Chicago, IL 60606

Compliments of
SSP

The
Engaging
Leader

Winning with Today's
Free Agent Workforce

Ed Gubman, Ph.D.

Dearborn™
Trade Publishing
A **Kaplan Professional** Company

Vice President and Publisher: Cynthia A. Zigmund
Editorial Director: Donald J. Hull
Senior Acquisitions Editor: Jean Iversen
Senior Project Editor: Trey Thoelcke
Interior Design: Lucy Jenkins
Cover Design: Gail Chandler
Typesetting: the dotted i

© 2003 by Ed Gubman

Published by Dearborn Trade Publishing, a Kaplan Professional Company

Printed in the United States of America

03   04   05   10   9   8   7   6   5   4   3   2   1

Library of Congress Cataloging-in-Publication Data

Gubman, Edward L.
    The engaging leader : winning with today's free agent workforce / Ed Gubman.
        p.   cm.
    Includes index.
    ISBN 0-7931-6514-8 (6X9 hardback)
    1. Supervision of employees. 2. Employee motivation. 3. Employee retention. 4. Leadership. I. Title.
HF5549.12 .G83 2003
658.3'02—dc21

2002155111

CONTENTS

Books are labors of love—you have to love writing to do the labor. Creating this book was a particular pleasure for me because it combined two of my passions—leadership and sports. I often look at leaders in business and sports through the same motivational lens.

I took this view a lot in my 17 years with Hewitt Associates. For the first 15 years there, I was building and leading a team—first a small one—then a global one, as a practice leader. Now I work independently, still consulting with executives about their teams. I can always find a good quote from Casey Stengel or a Zen inspiration from Phil Jackson to explain a situation or rally people's spirits.

During my last few years at Hewitt, we helped assist the people who worked with *Fortune* to select its list of the 100 best companies to work for in America. Working with this information, as well as personally with several of these companies, it became obvious to me that a particular kind of leadership, what I call "engaging leadership," lifted some companies to best employer status and left others as also-rans. I also realized that winning and losing with employees involved the same kinds of leader behaviors I saw in successful sports teams. Increasingly, great employees are like great athletes—they have choices about where and how hard to work, and their skills are in high demand. It doesn't matter what the unemployment rate is, there's always a shortage of talent to help your business win. This book describes engaging leadership.

Many people contributed to this book—especially the business executives with whom I've worked and watched lead. I'm also very appreciative of the great coaches who I've observed as a fan and the sportswriters who've depicted them. Two individuals deserve all-star mention. John Bausch, a prized colleague from my Hewitt days and a good friend, gave an early manuscript a close reading and suggested the framework that I ultimately used. John is a talented management consultant and business communicator, as well as a former sportswriter, so he was the perfect person to critique this work. My editors Jean Iversen, Don Hull, and their teammates at Dearborn Trade have been enthusiastic supporters of this project. What a great team to have on the field with me!

Above all, thanks and love to my wife Rachel and my two sons, Mike and Charlie, who are the inspiration for everything I do. (See, I wasn't just wasting my time watching all those games on TV.)

A DISENGAGED DISASTER

During the summer of 1999, I was reading about the collapse of the Colorado Rockies baseball team under manager Jim Leyland. Leyland came to Colorado as a high-priced savior, but he and the team never meshed. Things got so bad that he announced his resignation before the first season was over. This came as a mystery to the sports world, because Leyland was commonly referred to as a "baseball genius."

A genius in baseball is someone who gets more wins from his players than the payroll suggests. Leyland did this with a series of underpaid, overachieving Pittsburgh Pirates teams in the early 1990s. Claiming poverty like most small market teams—funny how St. Louis spends like a big market team and the Chicago teams pretend they're in small markets—the Pirates traded away their players when they became stars and could demand more money.

Eventually, Leyland got tired of seeing Barry Bonds, Bobby Bonilla, and other talents leave, so he followed them out the door.

He landed in Miami, where billionaire owner Wayne Huizenga promised to buy him a winning team. Huizenga was true to his word, and in 1997, Leyland led the Florida Marlins to the World Championship.

Baseball purists were shocked that Huizenga could do this so quickly, but Huizenga must have decided it was too easy. After all, it took him decades to make his billions in the waste hauling and movie renting businesses, but only a few years to win the World Series. When he won in 1997 but lost money in the process and couldn't get a new, publicly funded stadium, Huizenga got rid of his star players and prepared to sell the team.

Maybe Leyland was a baseball genius, but his real smarts were in having an out clause put into his Florida contract. If Huizenga ever started acting like he owned the Pirates, Leyland could leave. That's how Leyland went to Colorado in 1999.

What struck me about Leyland's short tenure with the Rockies was that it was full of the same problems I see in many people in business and other organizations. Leyland wasn't *engaged* in his work anymore. He didn't have a strong attachment to his job or his team. Being disengaged, he couldn't engage his players. Leyland didn't fit with his new organization, and he already had realized his professional dreams, so he didn't have any new ones to motivate him in Colorado.

At one time Jim Leyland was a great manager. Still, his experience in Colorado helped me to realize that leaders in pro sports and in business deal with many of the same issues, especially today when we have free agents in both arenas.

From that day on I started reading the sports pages with a different set of eyes. Instead of just enjoying them as a sports fan, I started looking at them from the perspective of my work as a management consultant and business psychologist. I began to appreciate that you could learn an enormous amount about leaders and their performance and careers by rethinking the sports section. In fact, almost every day some new drama plays out in sports that highlights a lesson about leaders—both good and bad.

Above all, the characteristics that make an engaging and successful leader in business today are pretty much the same things that make a winning leader in sports. The great thing about sports is that you can see this on a public stage, and the outcomes are readily apparent. If you pay attention and know what to look for, it's right there for you.

This book explains how to be a winning leader, based on my work with executives for the last 25 years. Instead of just using business examples, I am going to use stories from professional sports. I think this makes the lessons fresh, fun, and easy to remember. Plus, there are plenty of great illustrations of what to do and what not to do. I use these ideas in my consulting with leaders, and they work wonders for my clients. Now you can make them work for you.

CHAPTER ONE

ENGAGING LEADERSHIP

"He thinks group, but he always sees individuals."

—Former Senator Bill Bradley, describing his friend Phil Jackson's coaching style[1]

THE THRILL OF VICTORY

Ever wonder why some teams just keep winning? Consider this:

- In October 2000, the majestic New York Yankees won the World Series against their hated crosstown rivals, the Mets. This was the Yanks' 26th championship, far more than any other baseball team, and more than any pro team in any sport. It was also the 4th time in five years that the Yankees won the Series, all under the calm and responsive leadership of manager Joe Torre. In 2001, an aging Yankees team made it to the World Series again, defeating powerful Oakland and Seattle teams before falling to a tremendously tough Arizona team in seven incredible games. The Yankees had the best record in baseball and made the playoffs again in 2002, losing in the first round. Torre's streak ranked with the best of the great New York teams throughout baseball history.

- In 1999, Phil Jackson took over the talented but troubled Los Angeles Lakers. Built around stars Shaquille O'Neal and Kobe Bryant since the 1996–1997 season, the team never meshed. It collapsed in the conference semifinals the season before Jackson arrived. Jackson brought his Zen persona, triangle offense, and coaching assistants with him to Los Angeles and won the NBA championship in his first year with essentially the same team. Even though O'Neal and Bryant fought for team leadership most of Jackson's second season, the coach righted things by the end. The Lakers won their division and went on a 15–1 run through the playoffs, the best in NBA history, to repeat as champions. The next year Jackson added his third straight championship with the Lakers to the six titles he won in Chicago.

- At the end of the 2000 baseball season, the Seattle Mariners said good-bye to free agent all-star shortstop Alex Rodriquez, who went to the Texas Rangers for the biggest contract in baseball history. It was the third year in a row Seattle lost an all-star and likely future hall-of-famer. Pitcher Randy Johnson left in 1998, and outfielder Ken Griffey, Jr. left after the 1999 season. Yet in 2001, a rebuilt Mariners team tied an 83-year-old major league record with 116 wins. Under wily manager Lou Piniella, the M's reinvented themselves to become a team of great speed, pitching, and defense. In recognition for his work, Piniella was voted AL Manager of the Year for the second time. Ultimately the M's lost to the Yankees in the American League Championship Series, but given the New Yorkers' remarkable run, that's no disgrace.

Still wondering why some keep winning? It's leadership.

Of course, Torre, Jackson, and Piniella would be the first to tell you it's not all about them. They'd say it's about the players—the talent, and they'd be right. As Casey Stengel said when asked about his remarkable World Series winning streak with the Yankees, "I couldna' done it without my players."[2] Torre doesn't win without Derek Jeter, Bernie Williams, and their talented teammates. Jackson won with Michael Jordan and Scottie Pippen in Chicago—the best duo to play together until O'Neal and Bryant came along. Piniella had Edgar Martinez, Ichiro Suzuki, and other stars on the Mariners.

But winning is about how leaders engage the talent on their teams to perform to its maximum capabilities. Torre won four World Series, including three in a row, in an era when players change teams constantly, and every year teams spent just about as much as the Yankees. The Lakers had the same players the year before Jackson arrived and couldn't get it done. Very few baseball experts picked Piniella's Mariners to win their division in 2001, let alone tie the mark for all-time wins. *Talent is wasted when it's not engaged.* In fact, the ability to engage talent is the main ingredient of skillful leadership today. This is true in sports and business, and it has never been as critical a success factor as it is now.

ENGAGING FOR SUCCESS

A leader is someone who can engage people for success. Engaged people are passionately committed. If you are a leader who engages your employees, your people have strong psychological, social, and intellectual connections to their work, your organization, and its goals.

When people are engaged, they love what they do and what you're trying to achieve. They feel valued and the workday goes by quickly for them. They'll gladly put in extra hours and effort to help you get where you want to go. They'll soar "above and beyond" to create greater quality and service. They'll brag about you and your organization to others—they're your best salespeople. And they'll commit to stay with you. It would take enormous offers to get them to leave, and even then they may not do it.

Think about the enthusiasm and commitment you feel when you're most engaged in your work. What could your team accomplish if everyone felt that way?

Engaged followers should be your goal, and the goal of every leader. Engaged people are more productive, produce higher quality, and show higher rates of retention. They display more pride in their companies and share that pride with others. They build customer loyalty. They attract other high-caliber people. You need all of these things to win.

So that's your target—engaging your people—and this book will help you hit it.

WHAT ENGAGING LEADERS DO

Is there a single secret to becoming an engaging leader? I don't think so. You have to do lots of things to engage people, and to make sure you have the right talent to engage. The closest I've seen to a good prescription for engagement is the quote from Bill Bradley about his friend Jackson that starts this chapter. "He thinks group, but he always sees individuals."[3] This is an apt description of the way to engage people today. *Point the group toward the goals you want to achieve, but spend a lot of your time catering to the unique needs of individuals in your group, particularly the most talented ones.* For years, this didn't matter so much because there were more than enough skilled people to go around. If a talented person didn't work out, you could replace him or her without too much trouble. Not so today. If you don't spend time caring for your talented people, they'll leave, you won't be able to replace them quickly or cheaply, and you'll miss out on significant opportunities.

To describe engaging leadership in detail, let's look more closely at leadership styles.

DRIVERS AND BUILDERS

A friend and colleague of mine, another sports fan who makes his living as a management consultant, once told me about something Tex Winter said. Winter, a legendary basketball coach and close colleague of Phil Jackson's, noted that there are two kinds of coaches—*drivers and builders*. Though they might make strange bedfellows, Winter's description is just like that of Douglas McGregor. More than 40 years ago, McGregor, the well-known MIT management professor and business author, wrote his classic book about Theory X (drivers) and Theory Y (builders) managers.[4] Some very recent work at the Harvard Business School used quite similar types to describe companies, based on how they were led.

There are many more sophisticated ways to describe leaders, but this one is simple and has passed the test of time. Leaders do fall into these two categories pretty naturally, and their followers talk about them this way. It's often the first thing I see in a new client situation when I'm working with executives and their teams. Most leaders aren't "pure" types, but some are.

Drivers:

- *Put results first.* They want things done their way, and they want them done now.

- *Stress economic value above everything else.* Financial results top their lists.

- *Make the decisions.* They like being decisive and in control so they set the agenda and make as many decisions as possible.

- *"Crack the whip."* They keep the pressure on for accountability and come down hard when goals aren't met.

- *Focus on "what" and "when."* They want to know *what* have you done for me lately and *when* can I expect those results on my desk.

- *Take a short-term focus.* The day's, week's, or quarter's results are what matter.

- *Get "in your face" a lot.* They thrive on confrontation and let you know right away when you aren't performing.

- *Are more critical than positive.* They're hard to please and take delight in pushing you for more all the time; you can never do enough.

Pat Riley, coach of the Miami Heat, is a notorious driver. He pushes himself and his players hard, nonstop. That's the only way he believes in coaching. When forward A.C. Green played for the Heat, he said of Riley, "You never satisfy coach."[5] Builders are the opposite of drivers.

Builders:

- *Put people and processes first.* It's crucial to them that relationships are good and people feel involved. They believe this leads to results.

- *Stress organizational capabilities.* They want to build systems and talent and will sacrifice some financial gain to do it.

- *Get others involved.* They seek lots of input into decisions and delegate them as much as possible because they think that makes better decisions.

- *Let solutions emerge.* They don't try to tackle every problem right away. They believe the best solutions arise naturally and some problems solve themselves or go away.

- *Focus on "who" and "how."* The want to know *who* is affected or should be involved in a situation and *how* the issue was resolved in the proper way.

- *Take a long-term focus.* They're concerned about positioning their teams for success a year or two down the road.

- *Stay "behind the scenes" more.* They let their employees take center stage.

- *Are more positive than critical.* They practice the old saying of "you catch more flies with honey than with a fly swatter."

A classic builder is a "player's coach." Dennis Green, formerly of the Minnesota Vikings, is the perfect example. He let his players do their thing, and that's how he got them to buy into his agenda. They loved it, and it worked for years. Before he resigned, when there was talk of firing him, his temperamental star receiver Randy Moss said, "I can tell you that, straight up, if there were another coach, I probably wouldn't want to play here."[6] When Green left on his own terms, Moss reconsidered.

You can be quite successful as a driver or a builder, as long as you do it well and communicate effectively. *Communication is the fundamental leadership skill for everyone now.* But you won't be a consistent champion today if you just stay within your style. Both Riley and Green are winners—Riley has championship rings, and Green's teams got to the playoffs almost every year. They have records other coaches envy. Yet since they rely too heavily on their primary styles, they don't win it all anymore. They limit themselves by not expanding their behaviors.

Riley hasn't won a conference or NBA championship since the 1987–1988 season, when he worked with a whole different generation of players. For the last several seasons, Miami has been beaten early in the playoffs by lower ranked teams. After the Charlotte Hornets swept his higher seeded Heat in the first round of the 2000–2001 playoffs, he said he probably should be fired. Lucky for him, he was president and coach of the team, and the president didn't feel like firing the coach. In 2002, the Heat didn't even make the playoffs.

Green took the Vikings to the playoffs in eight of his first nine years as coach. He won four Central Division titles and in 1998 and 2000 coached heavily favored teams in the NFC Championship game, only to lose them both. The 2000 team lost the title in one of the most lopsided games ever, 41–0, to an unknown and underdog New York Giants team. The team was emotionally devastated afterwards, and it never recovered.

My lesson for leaders here is that neither Riley nor Green is *versatile* enough. Riley doesn't stop driving long enough to let his players catch their breaths and enjoy their achievements. Constant driving just grinds people down. It doesn't engage them. No wonder Riley's teams run out of energy at the end of the long NBA season. He pushes them so hard all year that they can't regroup, renew, and refocus to be successful in the playoffs. Because he's concentrating so heavily on short-term success, his playoff defeats have driven him to make big changes in team personnel every year. Under Riley, the Heat has to rekindle its chemistry annually. There's not enough continuity.

Green's teams had the opposite problem. The Vikings had trouble turning up the intensity for big games. Green took the same steady approach all the time and expected the players to motivate themselves. After all, isn't that the definition of a professional? Green rarely, if ever, "cracked the whip" so when the Vikings ran into a team that was really psyched, like the Giants in the championship game, they were overwhelmed right from the start. The Giants won that game in the first quarter. Randy Moss, Green's devoted fan, said even before kickoff he could tell the team wasn't ready, "I think all of our losses this year [2000] were because we were either too cocky or not up for the challenge. Nobody talked about coming out and smacking them in the mouth."[7] After the debacle of that game and the death of a key player the next season, Green simply lost control of some of his stars and, ultimately, the team.

Of course, you can find other faults in these cases, like Riley's complicated, slow-motion offensive style or Green's inability to build a strong defense. But if we stay focused on their leadership styles, we can see these coaches are limited because they rely too heavily on one approach. Strengths taken too far always result in weakness.

You also can find people who are ineffective with their styles: A driver who doesn't push hard enough for results but gets overly obsessed with details; a builder who is inclined to create strong relationships but lacks the emotional intelligence or interpersonal skills to make it happen. If you know what your style is, the first thing you need to do is develop it into a strength. *You can discover your style by taking the quick, self-scoring inventory at the end of this book.* Then, by using what's in this book, you can take the necessary steps to become more versatile. You may think drivers are more talkative and builders are more reserved. Sometimes that's true, but loud or quiet can go with either style. Success comes when you're communicating, whatever the volume. Torre and Jackson are quieter builders, while Green is more talkative. Piniella and Riley are extroverted drivers, but Bill Belichick of the New England Patriots is a more introverted driver who won the Super Bowl. You have to look across the range of behaviors I listed earlier to come to a correct categorization.

So, there are drivers and there are builders. Most people can't and don't change their basic leadership styles. Change happens very rarely and only after people go through some significant life event, like a great trauma, from which they learn a significant lesson. Even then, it's pretty unusual to change styles, and leaders really don't have to change to win.

ENGAGING LEADERS ARE VERSATILE

If overreliance on your basic style is a limitation, and people generally don't change, then what's a driver or builder to do? You could hire a second-in-command who complements your style, but that has its own set of issues. Instead, *you need to become more versatile.* You need to understand versatility, recognize situations where a departure from your usual approach will be more successful, and act accordingly. When you do this, you are better able to engage a broader variety of talents. You'll be able to guide a wider range of people and situations. This will make you more effective and successful. You won't change your basic style, but *you will use some of the best behaviors of the opposite style more often.* This isn't easy, but engaging leadership isn't supposed to be easy. That's why there are so few consistent winners among leaders.

Phil Jackson showed this versatility in bringing the Lakers together during the 2000–2001 season, but it was hard. For much of the year, O'Neal and Bryant fought each other over who was the team leader and Los Angeles played way below its potential. The infighting threatened to sink the entire season. Jackson tried to let them work it out by themselves. But even then, he scolded the two of them publicly and privately for their childlike behavior, calling it "silly" and likening it to a "sandbox fight." He also took Bryant aside to talk about trading him, while making it known that Shaq wasn't going anywhere.

Eventually, his comments got through to Bryant, who saw the team win without him while he was injured. Jackson thought the squabble forced a change in his coaching, "I'm much firmer with these guys. I was more lenient and patient last year than this year."[8] He didn't want to be. His inclinations as a builder were to let the two of them work it out, but he recognized he had to do something. Moreover, comments from the other Lakers showed they wanted Jackson to take control and solve the problem. They wanted him to lead.

In 2001, throughout baseball's long season, Lou Piniella showed a level of versatility that had been growing for several years. A fiery, hard-driving guy, Piniella was known early in his playing career for his temper and his toughness. Even as a manager in the late 1980s and early 1990s, he kicked his hat at umpires and trashed water coolers in the dugout. He pushed and prodded the 1990 Cincinnati Reds, with their "nasty boy" pitchers, to a surprising World Series victory. But age, maturity, and wisdom combined to calm him down. "I've really learned to manage since I've been here in Seattle," he says. "I manage myself and I manage my team better."[9]

Jay Buhner played for Piniella with both the Yankees and the Mariners. "We can remember his tirades, him kicking his hat and pulling up bases, and then, the next day, him coming in and he can't bend over because he pulled his back out trying to get the base out. He's still a very emotional guy. He wears his emotions on his sleeve. But he realizes he doesn't have to kick some of these guys in the butt. He's an absolute pleasure to work for and I would run through a wall for that guy."[10]

Drivers and builders become more engaging when they become more versatile and flexible in their approaches by adapting the best behaviors of the other style. *Engaging leadership is not a third style.* You're either a driver or a builder, and you're unlikely to change. But you become an engaging driver or an engaging builder when you learn to take on some good habits of the other style when it's necessary. The more you're able to do this, the more engaging you become. And the more engaging you become, the more you win.

As with Piniella, *engaging leadership usually is learned through experience.* Your natural inclination will be toward driving or building, but engaging people takes time and the wisdom you acquire by trying out different leadership approaches. Torre managed three different teams over 14 years and had a lifetime losing record before he got to the Yankees. Jackson was a player-coach, minor league coach, and assistant coach before taking over the Bulls. Some things take time and experience, and becoming an engaging leader is one of them.

What does versatility look like? We'll explore this throughout the book, but briefly:

- Drivers become more engaging when they become more patient, positive, and responsive to individual needs. They need to listen more and show greater concern for people, relationships, and processes. They become more engaging when they "dial down" the control, treat people like individuals, and trust them to do the right things.

- Builders become more engaging when they become more de-manding for results and accountability. They need to increase the pressure to get results and the appropriate consequences when the results are not met. They become more engaging when they insist people get with the program by putting aside their own agendas, and trust that people can handle the heightened demands.

As a result of being more versatile, engaging leaders in business:

- *Get their results through people.* They know that's how to win consistently.

- *Stress results and reinvestment.* They push hard for profitability and growth, in part so they can make sizeable reinvestments in developing people and organizational systems that enable people to work better.

- *Make the big decisions.* They make the big or tough decisions on a timely basis with a useful amount of input. They know followers expect them to lead. They also leave decisions about execution to the people closest to the work.

- *Intervene when appropriate.* They develop a feel for stepping in at the right times, not too often or too seldom. They know when to press hard to solve a problem or demand greater performance, and they know when to let people work things out on their own.

- *Focus on the head, hands, and heart.* They understand that getting work done requires head and hands, but more gets done when it is fueled by a love of the work. They make sure that people enjoy what they do and feel respected. This often involves finding out what the person wants to do and enabling them to do it.

- *Balance the short term and long term.* They keep one eye on the present and one on the future. They're quick to take action to address what's necessary for today while continuing to build for tomorrow.

- *Are "in the moment."* They vary between stepping front and center and hanging back, depending upon the situation. They'll shield their team if necessary or encourage team members to take the stage and the credit.

- *Show their feelings.* They express their emotions in an authentic and respectful way. Some leaders show a lot of emotion, others show less because of their personalities. But engaging leaders know the value of displaying their feelings. Your people learn to understand and expect your rhythms because they're real and out in the open. Engaging leaders are much more positive than negative because people respond better to that. They know the most important emotion is hope—hope is the wellspring of motivation. Still, they recognize they have to be realistic too. They can be effective when they're angry or critical as long as it's genuine and happens less frequently than joy, optimism, and praise.

Quarterback Trent Green summed up the description of an engaging leader when he described his coach in St. Louis and Kansas City, Dick Vermeil. Said Green, "Dick is such a positive and upbeat [person], always finding the best in a certain situation and always trying to stay real positive. He's not afraid to scream and yell, don't get me wrong, but for the most part he tries to keep everything positive. He's very demanding in terms of the amount of hours we have to spend and as much work as we do on the field."[11]

ENGAGING IMPACTS

When you display these behaviors, you engage your employees in several ways.

- You enable them to get to know you.

- You show them that you care about them.

- You help them admire you and want to work for you.

- You show them you're intensely passionate and optimistic about your work and your goals.

- You help them understand the value of taking a disciplined approach to performing.

Exposure and Knowledge

Today, you have to expose yourself to your people in ways leaders never had to before. The old, formal, distant, hierarchical-based idea of leadership is dying. Your talented people expect to relate to you in a more informal, egalitarian way, even if you would prefer to have it another way.

One of the best examples of this I ever encountered was an entrepreneurial leader I know who built a multibillion dollar technology company. When the packing and shipping line went down, he'd head straight to the warehouse to help put machines in boxes. When he wasn't needed for packing, he'd stay in the warehouse anyway, making sure people had the supplies they needed and coffee and food to keep going. Gordon Bethune did a similar thing in rebuilding Continental Airlines. He'd work the ticket counters and tarmacs on a regular basis.

On the other hand, one of the biggest weaknesses I see in some business leaders is that they keep their distance from their employees. I don't mean their fellow executives; I mean the people who serve customers, load boxes, think up marketing campaigns, enter data, and so on. How can you expect to know how customers are being served or how much quality goes into your products if you don't know what people are thinking and feeling? Teams take on the personalities of their leaders. Do you want yours to be cold, distant, and uncaring?

People expect to get to know who you really are—your personality and your preferences. That's why engaging leaders show their true feelings. They understand people want closeness. You shouldn't keep your distance, even if your employees want to keep their distance from you.

Employees also expect you to get to know them. David Grainger, who built W.W. Grainger into the United States' largest industrial and office supply business before retiring, was famous for walking the halls and distribution centers, remembering people by name, asking them about their families, and recalling their celebrations. That's one reason he became a beloved leader.

Sports have an advantage over many businesses in this regard: most sports teams and organizations are small so it's easy to get to know people. On the other hand, it's impossible for a coach to hide his weaknesses as a person. If you lead a small organization or work team, you must get to know your people personally—their families, hobbies, interests, and issues. In a large organization, it may be impossible for you to do that, but everyone can get to know you if you reveal your true self. You have to be authentic; people can sense when you are trying to be something you're not. By the way, if people don't like what you reveal, they'll tell you. Today, if you don't change, they'll probably tell you on your way or their way out the door.

Relationship Building and Caring

What I'm describing is *relationship building*, and as you build that relationship, you have to show you care. People aren't going to care about you and your concerns unless they know you care about theirs. General Colin Powell said, "The day soldiers stop bringing you their problems is the day you stopped leading them."[12]

Engaging leaders don't do this just to be nice, though it's the right way to deal with people. They do it because *the more caring they show, the more performance they can demand.* Think about it. For whom are you more likely to extend yourself, someone you love or someone you don't know or don't like?

In 1998, the Center for Creative Leadership did a study on what distinguishes effective leaders from ineffective ones. After reviewing mountains of data it found only one difference: effective leaders cared about their people.[13]

Demonstrating caring is done one on one. That means knowing what each member of your team needs to make him or her feel valued. Appreciation is a highly personal thing. It's different for each individual. To show appreciation, you may have to take as many different approaches as you have unique people. Your people will feel appreciated based on the personal relationship you build with each of them as their leader.

Dusty Baker, formerly of the San Francisco Giants, now the manager of the Cubs, won baseball's Manager of the Year award three times. He knows the way to a player's heart is through his stomach. Giants' star, Barry Bonds, gave away Baker's secret to success. "He always brings food in every day. He takes care of everybody. When he knows you're down and out, he does something to perk you up. When you're struggling, he'll say, 'Here I brought you lunch. You're looking a little weak. I want you to get strong.'"[14]

Baker learned the value of good nutrition from Hank Aaron and now spends $50 to $60 a day on food for his team. He knows every good restaurant in National League cities—not the fanciest, just the best. But he doesn't deliver food just to make people happy, he does it to win. "You've got to be nutritionally strong. In the end, only the strong survive."[15]

Phil Jackson feeds players egos, not their bodies. Former player Stacy King didn't get along well with Phil when they were with the Bulls. Now a coach in the CBA, King patterns himself after Phil. Said King, "During my first two years with him, I despised about 95 percent of Phil's approach. Now I see the big picture that I didn't see before. My style is actually a lot like Phil's, especially how he handled players. They all have personalities, and to mesh them together without too many restrictions on them takes a lot of work."[16]

Jackson discovered that Shaquille O'Neal wanted a close, father-son type relationship because of O'Neal's family background. So that's what Jackson worked on, even before he started coaching him. He also joined with O'Neal's family to encourage him to finish his degree. O'Neal, with the Lakers' blessing, left the team for a few days during the 2000–2001 season to attend graduation ceremonies at LSU. To Jackson, it was a matter of supporting O'Neal and his family and getting priorities right.

Admiration and Integrity

The ability to make smart, tough decisions, while still acknowledging the emotional side of things and responding to people's feelings, makes you a hero to your people. And *people want to work for leaders they admire.* I hear this all the time in my consulting. Employees spend a lot of time looking upward in their companies, and when they talk about bosses they admire—whether it's their supervisors or the CEO—they say it with a smile and great personal pride.

The desire to admire may be a distinctly American trait. I'm not certain. Some experts talk about Americans being hero worshippers, based on our culture that celebrates individualism. At the same time, much of the literature on leadership says that heroic leadership is overrated and unnecessary in organizations, even though that's what the business press likes to write about.

I agree you don't need to be a heroic leader, like the classic stereotype, to be a success. Still, you have to want to lead and be willing to get out in front. You don't have to be particularly charismatic, though you have to be able to communicate. People love and are inspired by everyday heroes. It helps them feel like they're working in the right company if they can look up to their leaders.

Arthur Ashe, the great tennis player, described very well the kind of hero to which I'm referring. Ashe said, "True heroism is remarkably sober, very undramatic. It is not the urge to surpass all others at whatever cost, but the urge to serve others at whatever cost."[17] *Leading by serving others to reach your organization's goals is the essence of engaging leadership.*

When I ask people what traits they most admire in leaders, the first thing they say is *integrity.* There are many other traits that people admire in their leaders, but integrity appears to be the foundation—courage, confidence, and caring all flow from it.

Integrity is a big word that can mean many different things. But keep it simple. If people are going to follow your lead, they expect you to act honestly and ethically. We've all seen what happens to a company when its leaders lack integrity—Enron comes to mind. The best people, the kind you want to keep, won't hang around if you do one thing and say another or don't play fairly.

People watch this very carefully all the time. Former New York mayor Rudy Giuliani earned everyone's overwhelming admiration for his leadership during the World Trade Center crisis. Though his political career was near ruin before September 11, after the horrible terrorist attack he showed the combination of toughness and tenderness that marks great, engaging leaders. People saw an authentic, emotional side to him that hadn't been visible before, and they were uplifted by it.

The one time he slipped in people's eyes was when he proposed staying on as mayor after New York City's November 2001 election. New Yorkers were highly critical of him because they saw this as a violation of the integrity of the election process. Once he dropped his ill-thought case for staying in office, New York's new love for him quickly returned.

Passion and Intensity

Your people also won't give you outstanding effort unless they see great *passion* from you. If it's not tremendously important to you, don't expect it to be very important to your team. Your team will take on your characteristics. If you want intensity and enthusiasm from your people, show them yours. If you're not prepared to work harder and longer than your people, you can't ask for maximum effort and quality from them. Engaging leaders ask and get people to work as hard as they do.

The Cleveland Browns, an expansion team, fired coach Chris Palmer after its first two seasons, hardly enough time to get started. When asked why, Browns' president Carmen Policy said, "I think football is almost as much feel and emotion as it is execution. A team will never grow unless it has spirit, energy, direction, and hope. And I think we were lacking a great deal of each of those."[18] Policy replaced Palmer with Butch Davis, a much more emotional and optimistic coach, and the Browns improved right away.

Is there an appropriate level of passion or intensity for a given type of business? I think so. Here the sports analogy fits again. Football has a relatively shorter season than baseball or basketball, and it's a collision sport. There are fewer games, but a football coach asks his players to do lots of dirty work and unnatural things— wear lots of padding, hit people hard, tackle other players who are running at you at full speed, play in all kinds of weather, and so on. This probably takes more pure emotion—executed at a louder volume—and a driver mentality. Drivers coached the last several Super Bowl winners. There are no dynasties anymore in football because of the salary cap, increased movement of players, the impact of the draft, and a scheduling process that rewards weaker teams by giving them easier schedules. So football has a shorter-term focus: A team gets a two or three year window to win it all. This helps explain why an engaging driver, like Dick Vermeil or Brian Billick, wins and Dennis Green falls short.

Still, the newer coaches in the NFL, with a few exceptions, tend to be teachers more than screamers. They're calmer, but if they're versatile, they have their loud moments. Steve Marriuci, the successful coach of the San Francisco 49ers, described his approach, "I think you can be a gentleman and succeed and treat players fairly and like men."[19] The hardcore screamers, like Mike Ditka, have faded into the past.

Basketball and baseball seasons, on the other hand, are a longer grind in which the teams play almost every day for seven months with fewer people. This requires a steadier approach, more like the builder mind-set. As Steve Kerr, a long-time NBA player with several teams said, "I think it's difficult as a player when you've got a coach jumping up and down on the sidelines all the time. You feel more relaxed when your coach is relaxed."[20]

In my experience, businesses that are more operationally focused, where the activities are more repetitive, controlled by processes, group-oriented, and perhaps less intellectually stimulating, are more like football. They require more passion from the top for employee motivation, and effective and engaging drivers can do well. Many manufacturing and process-driven companies, like Whirlpool or Southwest Airlines, benefit from this kind of leadership. So do customer service companies that involve short-cycle sales or more straightforward service operations, like FedEx or Wal-Mart. Though there may be less intrinsic motivation in the work itself, you need to provide more inspirational leadership throughout the company. This requires more volume and outward emotion from you and other leaders.

When work is more individually focused and personally and intellectually challenging, like engineering, legal work, health care, and consulting, or the emphasis is on long-term, carefully cultivated relationships, the calmer approach is better. In companies like Merck or IBM, you can appeal to the person on an individual level about issues of quality, service, and the other results you need. Leadership doesn't usually require the same volume, and highly aggressive leaders often are counterproductive. They become a distraction to the thinkers who are creating products and relationships. A builder is a more effective leader in these types of companies.

Still, the importance of communicating passion can't be overstated for any kind of work. Both cold drivers and calm builders have to change their approaches. Your passion, as long as it's positive, unlocks the energy that fuels people to victory. Without passion, you can't have quality. People want passion and hope in their lives, and talented people want to feel it in their jobs.

At the same time, engaging leaders know the difference between intensity and tension. They raise the tension just enough to have intense motivation. Too much tension becomes its own focus and causes distraction. This is the downfall of many drivers who can't move beyond their usual style. On the other hand, builders who aren't versatile seem not to create enough tension or they inadvertently cause too much. When they don't create enough, their people lack the fire that it takes to win. When they effect too much tension, it's because they let a problem go unresolved for too long. Their followers feel overly tense because they're waiting nervously for their leader to help with the problem.

Your task as an engaging leader is to create just enough intensity so people can enjoy their work every day. People need to have fun to win. You can actually measure whether the intensity level is right by how much people love what they do. Tense or fear-oriented leadership takes the fun out of it for everyone. As Lou Piniella says, "Basically, I let my players play. I want them to have fun, I want them to be relaxed and loose and go out and give me all they've got. When players execute, it makes the manager look good."[21]

If the proper intensity is there most days and you've built strong relationships with your team, you can turn up the intensity when you need to rise to a challenge or make big changes. You can ask for more and get it during big moments. You can ask people to extend themselves even further than they think they can. They'll reach for the impossible and do it when they're able because you've engaged them.

Discipline and Participation

The last fundamental for an engaging leader is to *set a discipline for performing.* In some ways, this comes easily for both drivers and builders, though they approach it differently. How things get done is very important to both of them—for drivers it's often "my way" and for builders it's "let's agree on how to do it?" Ineffective leaders rely too much on their own usual approach—either "my way or the highway" or "you people decide and let me know." Engagers understand it's a combination of both top-down direction and bottom-up involvement. They know when to make the decision, how much input to get, and when to let others decide. People need to buy in to what you want to get done, but they won't accept it unless they have a voice in goals and methods.

Engage people by establishing accountabilities and a structure for accomplishing them, and then let them operate. This may seem obvious after all these years of employee involvement, but I still see many companies grind people down with operational efficiencies, driving pride and creativity out in the name of process control. Varying processes does disrupt efficiency, but a lack of opportunity for input just puts people to sleep. You need to strike a balance between prescribed methods and enabling employees to have their say, or you can watch your productivity fall as dullness overcomes your workplace.

Engaging leaders balance the right fundamentals for playing their games or running their businesses with the right level of participation by their team members. During the 2001 baseball play-offs, Piniella's Mariners got beat by Cleveland in game four by a score of 17–2. Piniella hated to lose but he wasn't upset with the score. Instead he was concerned because his team didn't play good defense. He didn't scream after the embarrassing loss because he knew his veteran team would steady themselves. His players took it upon themselves to go into their locker room to sit and talk it over. They said they spent most of the hour kidding each other and laughing, forgetting about how badly they played, so they could get ready for the next game. It must have worked. The Mariners won the decisive fifth game to go on to the League Championship.

Phil Jackson surprised people at how quickly he was able to take the same Lakers team all the way to the top after it collapsed in the playoffs the previous year. Even the man who replaced him with the Bulls, Tim Floyd, was impressed with the structure Jackson brought, "He [Jackson] did a remarkable job of organizing that team, identifying and giving them roles, identifying who their shot-makers were, shoring up their defense, teaching them how to play playoff basketball, the whole deal."[22]

These behaviors—learning about your people, relationship building, caring, integrity, passion, and discipline—form the foundation of engaging leadership, whether you're a driver or a builder. When you read positive comments about coaches from their players, these are the things players almost always describe. What would your team say about you?

People who watched Bill Belichick lead the New England Patriots to the Super Bowl Championship said he changed and grew as a leader. He was still the same defensive mastermind, but he was no longer so aloof and remote, a communications disaster. This was his second try at being a head coach, and he learned to loosen up and listen more. One of his players, Terrell Buckley, said, "The great coaches listen to their players but keep control. That's when you have something special. It makes players around here excited."[23]

Tough and tender. A loveable taskmaster. Realistic optimist. Whatever you call it, the intersection of driving and building behaviors is what engages most people. Successful leaders learn this in their interactions with people. They become more versatile, expanding their own styles by taking on some behaviors that are unnatural to them at first, but become second nature as followers reinforce them by responding favorably. The ability to incorporate parts of these seeming opposites, like the skill of reconciling group goals and individual needs, will make you an engaging leader and a long-time, big-time winner.

THE HUDDLE

1. Now that you've read about drivers and builders, what's your style? How do you know? (Complete the short questionnaire at the end of this book to find out.) Which coaches or leaders do you most admire? What are their styles? Usually you admire people who are like you or the ones you want to be like.

2. How versatile are you? Do you regularly use behaviors of both drivers and builders? Which behaviors? What do your people say about you? How engaging do they think you are?

3. Answer the following questions using a 1-to-5 scale, with 5 being a high score:

   • How well do you get to know your people?

   • How successfully do you show your people you care about them?

- How much do your people admire you?

- How often do you display your passion and optimism for your work and your goals?

- Do you bring a disciplined approach to getting things done the right way?

What do you need to do to bring each score up to a 5?

CHAPTER TWO

THE URGENCY OF ENGAGEMENT

"If Phil goes, I'm right behind him. At this point in my career,
I couldn't play for anyone else."

—All-Star center and MVP Shaquille O'Neal on his coach, Phil Jackson[1]

MARKET-DRIVEN EMPLOYMENT RELATIONSHIPS

You'll notice that the quote from Shaq is just like the quote in the previous chapter from Randy Moss about Dennis Green. Great leaders inspire that kind of loyalty. And, engaging leaders win.

There's an urgency to becoming an engaging leader that never existed before. You must become more engaging, and you should do it right away. It's not just that engaging leaders win; it's the changing nature of business and the workforce. You have to become an engaging leader if you want to get and keep the talent you'll need to achieve the results you want.

We now live in an era of unprecedented volatility in labor markets. Like it or not, and there are many reasons not to like it, just-in-time workforces are the rule. For example, in one year, from October 2000 to October 2001, we spun from the tightest labor market in recent history—employers couldn't find people to hire no matter what they offered—to widespread panic over layoffs. We lost over 1.5 million jobs in the United States during this period as business slowed down, and even profitable companies cut jobs and people.

Though there's evidence that avoiding layoffs is good for business, fewer companies seem to acknowledge or practice this, and sometimes layoffs do seem unavoidable. Laying off people to cut costs occurs more widely with each dip in the business cycle. Some companies now get rid of people just because profits aren't growing fast enough. No wonder our workforce is wary and distrustful.

The laws of supply and demand rule labor markets today, just like they do markets for money and goods. This wasn't always the case. Until the early 1980s, many companies shielded employees from downturns because that was how they maintained loyal workforces. No more. Since then we've built a market-driven employment relationship, where the workplace and the outside marketplace move hand in hand. When business is slow and jobs are scarce, power and resources belong to employers. When business is good and jobs are plentiful, employees have the power.

Guess what? Talented employees are about to gain more power than ever. You'll need them more than they'll need you.

THE COMING TALENT SHORTAGE

Here's a dire warning for business leaders: The demand for skilled talent is about to far outstrip the supply, and stay that way. Even during the downturn and recession of 2000–2002, unemployment stayed low by historical standards. There were shortages of skilled people in some industries and parts of the country. These shortages are going to spread and increase, even when the economy isn't booming.

Talent shortages will become a way of life for you and your business. Think of October 2000, when unemployment hit 3.9 percent nationwide, as a preview of things to come. Quite soon you'll feel like you're in a permanent talent shortage, always challenged to get the people you need. As management guru Peter Drucker said about the new workforce, "Accept the fact that we have to treat almost anybody as a volunteer."[2]

Demographics and Skills

The reason for this is primarily *demographic*. The U.S. workforce is growing very slowly. Soon it will actually shrink for several years before it returns to another period of slow growth. The talent pool won't be able to keep up with employment needs and you'll have trouble hitting your business goals.

It's a matter of numbers. There were about 77 million people born between 1946 and 1964—the baby boom generation. But there were only 52 million people born between 1965 and 1978—generation X. This means you'll see a huge drop-off in the number of people who are in their prime working years, ages 21 to 60, over the next few years as baby boomers start to retire. In fact, the most conservative projections, based on U.S. Department of Labor numbers, tell us that by 2006, when the first boomers turn 60, there will be two million more jobs in this country than people to do them. By 2011, the shortage will be five million people.[3]

Even in a slow economy, we'll still have a shortage of talented people. The Department of Labor numbers only assume a moderate growth rate in the gross domestic product, quite a bit slower than we had during our long economic expansion from 1992–2000. So, the actual talent shortage could be much bigger. Some demographers and economists think it may grow as large as 10 million people over the next 20 years.

When will you see relief? Not for a long time. Generation Y, largely the children of baby boomers, numbers about 78 million. The first of them are entering the workforce now, but most won't be educated and ready for years. By then, many of Gen Y's baby boom parents will be retiring, so their entry into the workforce won't ease the pain too much. All they'll do is replace the departing boomers.

In addition to the numbers, there's also the issue of *skills*. We aren't educating highly skilled people fast enough to keep up with the growing demands of our more complicated jobs. An increasing number of jobs now require the equivalent of a college education to perform them. Jobs that used to be simple now call for complex problem solving as more technology is put into use. Computers haven't made things simpler; they've made them more difficult. In ten years, the United States could have a gap of at least 3.5 million jobs requiring bachelor's degrees with no one to fill them.

Attitudes and Values

People's attitudes and values about work have changed too. *In market-driven employment relationships, the attitude of both companies and employees is "what have you done for me lately?"* Job hopping increases or slows down in sync with the economy, but even in bad times skilled people keep moving to better opportunities. This will only increase as the talent pool shrinks.

Indeed, many people no longer think about long-term jobs in organizations. Loyalty to organizations is pretty much dead in business. Corporate America killed it through layoffs, restructurings, mergers, and similar activities of the last 20 years. People have learned to fend for themselves.

Consider this:

- According to the Department of Labor, almost 40 percent of American workers have been with their companies two years or less. This is double what it used to be.[4]

- Less than 10 percent of American workers have been with their companies more than 20 years. This is about half of what it traditionally was.

- It used to be that, on average, people had three or four jobs during their careers. Now that number has grown to seven or eight, and it keeps growing as people become more mobile.

- Even companies on *Fortune* magazine's list of the 100 best places to work in America report average voluntary turnover of about 14 percent.[5]

- Department of Labor numbers suggest that about one-quarter of American workers are "free agents." They're self-employed or work temporarily or in very small businesses that employ just a handful of people. These free agents outnumber people that work in manufacturing or the public sector, the largest parts of the economy.

Surveys of American workers show repeatedly that while a large majority of people would like to be loyal to their employers, most know their loyalty will not be reciprocated.[6] They realize they'll be let go without much hesitation whenever the company wants. Most people now understand that job security doesn't exist and their career security depends on their skill set, not their companies. In addition, only about one-third of Americans love their jobs.

Workforce attitudes break out like this:

- About one-quarter to one-third feel real loyalty to their employers, defined as wanting to and expecting to stay at their companies for the next few years. This percentage is much higher for executives and much lower for rank-and-file employees.

- One-third feel "trapped." They'd like to leave their companies if they could, but they think it will be difficult to find another job. This feeling is strongest among younger baby boomers and generation Xers who have growing family responsibilities.

- Another one-third would leave their jobs tomorrow. The younger you are, the more likely you are to feel this way.[7]

Additionally, with big technology changes in the ways companies hire and the ways people look for jobs, today more than half of the workforce is constantly "scanning" for new opportunities— checking Web sites, posting resumes on the Internet, looking at Web-based job boards, and so on.[8] They also do things the old-fashioned way, talking to friends about where they work and answering calls from recruiters.

Companies may not like this, but it's probably the right mindset to have. It shows flexibility and self-preservation, just like the ways companies hire, fire, and pay people. Long-term employment has become a thing of the past for most. Pension plans, promotions, and annual pay increases have given way to defined contribution plans, flatter organizations, and variable pay, so reward schemes no longer bind people to companies. Benefit plans are portable and pay is contingent on performance. This is the market-driven employment relationship.

WHAT TALENT WANTS

The new realities of employment have fueled many of these attitude changes. Changes in *values* drive a lot of them too. Today baby boomers and gen Xers make up the bulk of the workforce, with gen Yers starting to join. Parents raised these generations with heavy emphasis on the individual. Though there are big differences between these three generations, it's fair to say that a large majority of them are looking for four things from work: *freedom, control, accountability, and caring.*

Freedom

Freedom means the ability to be who you are and express yourself without having to be someone you're not. Self-expression started with the boomers and grew stronger in succeeding generations. People expect to be able to voice their opinions, dress as they want within reason, and bring their personalities to work, not check them at the door. They also expect to be listened to and taken seriously by their bosses. Self-expression also stands for finding meaning in your work, or at least liking what you do. This is another key value of these generations. Finally, talented employees expect to have opportunities for development so they can keep learning and growing. They know this is really critical for their own personal career security in the permanently unstable working world.

Control

Demands for self-expression also lead to increasing expectations for *personal control* over work. People enjoy their work when they know what their responsibilities are and have the autonomy to achieve them. They don't want to be told what to do and how to do it. Even when the what-to-do comes down from above, talented employees expect to figure out how to do it themselves. You also see this in increasing demands for control over how people spend their time at work. Boomers were the first to ask for some flexibility in their work and lives. Gen Xers went further and asked for work-life balance. Gen Yers believe their work should reflect their true interests and unique personalities—work and life should be completely integrated. Corporations that try to fit them into cubicles will have lots of empty spaces.

Accountability

Accountability means giving someone an assignment and holding him or her responsible for delivering results. This isn't unique to these generations but it's heightened in them. It's part of the spirit of free agency, of working for yourself. Talented people want this because they believe performance is the only guarantee for their futures. Paternalism and protected employment are dead, so the attitude is "give me the chance to perform and hold me accountable so I can show you what I can do." In fact, one sure way to tell if you've got high-initiative, high-talent employees is to see if they want to be accountable. When people shrink from accountability, they'll want you to take care of them and assure they'll be okay even when they don't deliver. Who wants employees like that?

Caring

Caring relationships increase people's investments in your workplace. Warm relationships help employees feel connected, like who they are matters. This multiplies their motivations to help you meet your goals. Employees who like their associates will want to do well for their friends, coworkers, and you. They also want people they can talk to about personal things at work, others to confide in about their issues. For some of that, they'll come to you, if they feel safe. For the rest, they want some friends. A sure sign of disengagement, as well as poor social skills, is when a person doesn't have close relationships at work.

Freedom, control, accountability, and caring are ways for people to seek some measure of individual stability in a very unstable and constantly changing world. They help people feel like they're important and that they're working for themselves. This is the best of the free agent mind-set, and what you want your employees to feel. The more they sense these things, the more they'll feel they've chosen to work for you. *Choice may be the most powerful motivator of all.*

Perceived choice also increases people's sense of self-reliance, because they think they did it themselves. When all you see around you is impermanence, you have to become your own anchor. Think about the work experience of gen X. When it started to enter the workforce in the late 1980s and early 1990s, it hit tough job markets, fed by restructuring employers and uneven economic times. Then when things started to boom in the mid-1990s, Xers were in such hot demand, they could name their own terms. When the slowdown hit in 2000, they saw their jobs evaporate, particularly in the technology sector. No wonder they learned to fend for themselves.

Respond to These Values

To engage people, you have to respond to these attitudes and values. You can't impose a "one size fits all" command and control approach. You have to give people room to feel they're making their own decisions about how to do their jobs and the amount of effort to put into them. At the same time, you can't be too lax or you won't be successful. People in organizations want structure; if they didn't, they'd be out working on their own. Yet people still want to feel the pride associated with being successful. It takes standards to get there. You have to adapt and hit the right balance.

This is one reason hardcore drivers like Pat Riley don't win as much anymore. Many drivers don't provide enough room for individuals to feel like they're making their own choices. Riley was born at the end of the last generation to emphasize teamwork and sacrifice individualism for duty. This is the "Ike" generation, born between the end of the Great Depression and the end of World War II and named after war hero President Dwight Eisenhower. As children, they grew up watching America, led by big government, rise up out of financial disaster, defeat the Axis powers, and rebuild much of the world after the war.

Seeing this, Ikes learned to trust institutions, making it the last generation to put the corporation first, ahead of home and family. No surprise that the team movement in American business hit its peak while Ikes were CEOs. But for Ikes or anyone else to win today they need to adapt. Riley's methods worked well when he was coaching older boomers, like Magic Johnson and Kareem Abdul Jabbar, who still could be taught to buy into his way of thinking.

People feel very differently today, especially Xers and Yers. They don't trust government, business, or other institutions, including your company. They don't see stability in them; they live change. They believe personal security comes from trusting their own instincts and abilities. We might yearn to go back to a simpler time, but it's not reality. Riley's now coaching Xers and Yers, but he hasn't changed to accommodate their different beliefs. It's no surprise he doesn't like playing rookies on his teams and only does so when there's no alternative.

Still, hard-driving, command-and-control leadership is not just the province of the Ike generation. A funny thing happened to Buck Showalter on the way to the 2001 World Series. He had managed and helped build the two teams that competed, the Yankees and the Arizona Diamondbacks, but he wasn't leading either of them in the series. Showalter is a baby boomer who's every bit as hard-driving as Riley. His organizational manual for the Diamondbacks was thick and rule-bound, just like Riley's playbook. Showalter even told players how high to wear their socks. In New York and Arizona, Showalter built his teams and got them to the playoffs, but lost in the first round. Then he was fired from both places for being too controlling. Each time a more laid-back person—Joe Torre in New York and Bob Brenly in Arizona—replaced him, and each time the team won the World Series the next year.

Quite telling was Brenly's first big move after taking over Arizona. When training camp opened, he gathered all the players together. He took Showalter's big manual and dropped it to the floor. In its place he took out a napkin and wrote down his rules: Play hard and be on time. His players followed them and became the fastest expansion team to win the World Series.[9] Brenly clearly understood how to engage people by giving them the freedom to succeed.

ENGAGING LEADERSHIP IS THE SOLUTION

No one knows where these huge changes in the employment relationship, the talent shortage, or new attitudes and values will take us, but one thing is apparent: For the foreseeable future, *talented people won't stay in jobs they don't like.* They'll have more opportunities than ever, and they won't stay with their companies if they can't stand their bosses. As the old saying goes, "people don't quit their jobs, they quit their bosses." This is truer today than ever. Lousy leaders will run the stars out of your companies.

On the other hand, there's plenty of evidence to suggest that skilled people want to work for winning leaders. Grade A talent wants to work for Grade A leadership. It won't settle for less. *You can build loyalty to engaging bosses, even if you can't build it to companies.* Stars like Shaquille O'Neal can play anywhere. He's already played for two teams and several coaches, but he loves playing for Jackson. To be an engaging leader, you need to figure out how Phil Jackson and others like him build this kind of devotion.

For three years, I helped lead Hewitt Associates in gathering and analyzing the data that *Fortune* magazine used to publish in its list of the 100 best places to work in the United States. Several factors contributed to a company making the list. The number one factor was leadership. Leaders who emphasized inspiring and engaging people were the keys to being a great employer. These leaders knew they had to manage relationships, as well as the bottom line, to have lasting success. With this kind of leadership, these companies had twice the applicant pool and half the turnover of other companies.

The lesson for you is you have to develop your skills at engaging people whether you manage in a for-profit business, a not-for-profit organization, or even lead volunteer work in your church or community. The opportunities available to talented individuals and the demands placed on them will keep them very, very busy in the years ahead. As a leader, you will face huge challenges in getting and holding skilled people—bigger obstacles than you've ever experienced before.

You'll have to navigate your way through these rough waters, and you'll need some kind of compass. Very few employers have been here before, and there's no proven business model showing how to do it. You have to look somewhere else for clues.

That's why I picked pro sports as a way to illustrate engaging leadership. Sports have been dealing with a shortage of skilled talent, great mobility, and a workforce full of gen Xers and Yers for several years. Leadership in sports shows us some huge triumphs and some gigantic mistakes, so it's a great learning laboratory. When your best talent can change companies like Shaquille O'Neal can change teams, *the place to look to learn how to lead people today is professional sports.*

MIXING SPORTS AND BUSINESS

Does it really make sense to look at sports to learn about business leadership? Yes, because the worlds of professional sports and business never have been more similar, particularly when it comes to leading skilled, highly mobile talent.

I think you can learn a lot about effective leadership as we examine how a variety of individuals and organizations win. It's also undeniable that pro coaches and teams have made some spectacular mistakes in leading players. We'll look at some of these errors, along with the successes, to understand how you can become an engaging leader.

Just think about how much alike professional sports and business are now.

- Above everything else, talent now defines whether you win or lose. This always has been true in sports. It's true today in business where more than 80 percent of U.S. jobs are in the service and information industries. Value creation in these industries is mostly a matter of brain power and sharing information—in other words, talent and how it works together.

- Pro athletes and skilled employees both have unprecedented freedom of movement, and this will continue to grow. Athletes achieved this through strong unions, agents, and the premium placed on athletic skills. Employees are getting there due to the talent shortage and new technology.

- Loyalty has evaporated in both places. Corporations broke the loyalty bonds with their continual restructurings and layoffs. Free agency took care of it in sports. Comedian Jerry Seinfeld says players move around so much in sports that we're just rooting for the uniform now. In other words, we're all cheering for laundry.

- Because talent is so critical for success and so mobile, both sports and business now invest money and time more heavily in recruiting. Witness the wooing of free agents in baseball and basketball. Then look at how similar that is to what companies do on college campuses, particularly in knowledge-based industries. One Chicago law firm even rented out Comiskey Park to host a softball game between Northwestern and University of Chicago law students as a recruiting event. Moreover, sports and business both are looking at younger and younger talent, even reaching into high schools to find future stars. IBM and other companies sponsor a high school road show urging college-bound youngsters to major in technical fields so these companies will have a future talent pool.

- In both worlds, competitive pay is absolutely necessary to get the talent you want, but it's not sufficient. There's increasing evidence that great athletes and employees want more.

They want to play or work in successful organizations for terrific coaches. In some cases, they'll even turn down more money to go with a winner.

- There's much more media attention and pressure for short-term results in sports and business now. New cable channels, radio stations, and Internet sites are constantly emerging to discuss winners and losers. Not only that, but owners and shareholders are more impatient than ever.

Bill Parcells, former coach of the NFL's Giants, Patriots, and Jets, made the same comparison in the *Harvard Business Review,* when he was asked to discuss his approach to leadership. Parcells said, "The people in your company have little loyalty; some even want you to fail. Your star performers expect constant pampering. Your stockholders are impatient, demanding quick results. And the media scrutinize and second-guess your every move. I can relate."[10]

Still, sports and business aren't identical, and we should recognize some big differences.

- Unions now are stronger in pro sports than they are in most businesses. Unionization occurs only in about 10 percent of for-profit businesses, and their power is concentrated in a few segments, like transportation and the auto industry. Union membership is higher in not-for-profit segments, like education, health care, and government.

- Agents play a bigger role in sports than they do in business. Some people think agents have ruined pro sports. The use of agents is just beginning in business, but it's definitely coming. Some executive search and law firms are beginning to play this role for executives and uniquely skilled individuals.

- The compensation systems in pro sports leagues don't compare to business, and baseball, especially, seems completely broken. Most baseball teams report big operating losses year after year, even though franchises continue to increase in value. Yet as we've seen in the Enron, Tyco, and WorldCom cases, compensation systems in business aren't in great shape either, particularly the ways executives are rewarded. It's disgusting to see CEOs get fired for poor performance and walk away with millions. Say, that's a lot like baseball.

- Sports have defined seasons by which they measure success. Businesses have to measure success every day, though they have quarterly results to report. Sports team will do major makeovers in their off-seasons, but there's no off-season in business. Huge makeovers usually come during crises or mergers and acquisitions.

- Sports teams can get rid of players easily, while it's tougher to do that in business. Players can be traded or released, particularly when they're thought to be too old to perform. We have laws against that sort of thing in business.

These differences may seem huge to you, but the similarities are stronger than the differences, and the two are becoming more alike every day. As the business environment gets tougher, you need to take the best ideas about leadership wherever you can find them and use them to help you succeed. Your success depends on your abilities to get and keep star talents and engage them to help you win. You need to know how leaders who deal with scarce talent do this every day and triumph.

THE REST OF THIS BOOK

Now that I've defined engaging leadership, sketched the coming environment for talent, and told you why I think the analogy to sports works, here's what's next. The remainder of this book digs deeper into engaging leadership so you can build your understanding and learn how to do it. To do that, we'll focus on the three key areas where engaging leaders build successful teams. This isn't everything leaders have to do, but they are the most important things to do to become more engaging. I see this in business, sports, and every team endeavor. These three areas are:

- *Talent.* How you select, develop, and keep the talent you need to achieve high performance.

- *Goals.* How you excite people about your goals so they'll put in extra effort.

- *Chemistry.* How you build an environment with trust and structure so people can work together effectively and with excellence.

Drivers and builders have to address all three things to win. They approach them differently, and I'll point that out. Most crucial is for you to recognize how you do these things now and how you can become more versatile to engage your people.

Before we go any further, I acknowledge there's a lot wrong with professional sports. We all know it: greedy owners, coaches, and players; escalating prices that drive fans away; strange collective bargaining agreements that benefit the few at the cost of the many; thug-like behavior by some athletes; gross immaturity by others; unsavory agents; and so on. We've even reached the point where Super Bowl XXXV MVP, Ray Lewis, doesn't get asked to go to Disney World or appear in the team photo on the Wheaties box because of his off-the-field behavior. The only thing I can think of that may be worse is college athletics. The athletes make millions for their schools, don't get paid for it, and can't transfer without penalties, all while their coaches take off for richer jobs at the drop of a new shoe contract.

We can't ignore the bad in pro sports, but I really want to concentrate on those golden moments when a team comes together and wins. How did the coach engage his players to do it? How does an organization stay on top for years? What kind of leadership does that require? How come some teams never win? How do you avoid that trap? These are the things you can learn from and apply to your own skills to become more engaging and successful.

While you probably could understand all you need to know about leadership just by using the Yankees and Cubs as examples— after all, who typifies winning and losing more than those two teams—you'd be missing out on too many other great stories. Looked at through the right lens, pro sports provide a great picture of engaging leadership.

THE HUDDLE

1. Describe the employment relationships you have at your company. Do you practice layoffs or loyalty? Do you talk about one and do the other, or are your words and actions consistent? What impacts does this have on your workforce?

2. What are you doing to get ready for the coming talent shortage?

3. How in tune are you with the attitudes and values of your employees? How do you describe them? What generational differences do you observe? What similarities?

4. How have you modified your leadership style to address the employment relationships and attitudes and values that you described? How has this helped you lead? What should you do better?

3

TALENT

Get What You Need

*"Money or not, it still comes down to your ability
to evaluate talent."*

—Brian Sabean, San Francisco Giants general manager[1]

BUILD ON YOUR STRENGTHS

A fan asked Yankee coach Don Zimmer, "What makes Joe Torre such a good manager?" Zimmer replied, "Good players."[2] He was only half-serious. Zimmer knows you can't win without the right players, but he thinks Torre's a terrific manager. Still, not every coach wins with great talent.

The upside of our mobile economy is that talent will move in good times or bad. People will come to work for you when you offer the right inducements. One huge inducement is the opportunity to win.

Ernie Accorsi, general manager of the New York Giants said, "Because of free agency, players are here because they want to be here. It's not like you draft them, and they have no choice. They don't come here . . . if they don't think they have a chance to win."[3]

Highly skilled employees are just like free agents in sports. Your critical tasks are to know what you need to win and pick the best people who fit your team.

This begins with *understanding your strengths* and building on them. Certainly if your team has some glaring weaknesses—gaps in your skills or knowledge—correct them. But winning comes from concentrating on your strong points and building them to championship status. This forces you to focus on doing a few crucial things better than anyone else does—the things you have to do to win. This is the road to success. Trying to do everything well—being all things to all people—is too expensive, causes you to lose focus, and ultimately confuses your customers and employees who don't know what to expect from you.

This is one area where there isn't much difference between drivers and builders. It has nothing to do with style. You either get this concept or you don't. You'll be successful or you won't.

Sports may be a little easier to understand than business on this point because success models in sports are pretty constant. In baseball, the old adage is pitching is 80 percent of the game. This always proves true in the World Series. The team with the best pitching, smart defense, and just enough hitting wins. You may make the playoffs with a lot of hitting and just enough pitching, but no team slugs its way to win the World Series. It just doesn't happen.

It's basically the same in other sports. In football, basketball, and hockey, it's almost always the teams that play the best defense and have just enough offense that win championships. The St. Louis Rams were an exception to this rule because they won the Super Bowl with offense. On the other hand, the Denver Broncos, who won the two previous Super Bowls, didn't win throughout QB John Elway's brilliant career until they developed a stout defense and a great running game. The Baltimore Ravens and New England

Patriots, champions of Super Bowls XXXV and XXXVI, showed that brilliant defenses, even with mediocre offenses, win.

In business, there are many different ways to win, but the principle of focusing on your strengths is the same. Research on market leadership shows successful businesses emphasize their dominant value proposition to build their core competencies and drive those to become market leaders. You have to be competitive on price, product, and service, but you have to pick one of those values and use it to dominate your market. You do this by building your organization, systems, and talent to fulfill this dominant value proposition, the way Wal-Mart does on price, Nextel does on product, or the Four Seasons Hotel does on service.[4] Your business strategy, operating model, and goals should come from your dominant value proposition and help you get to the top.

Some rare companies are skillful enough to differentiate—be somewhat better than competitive—in a second area, like the way Southwest Airlines dominates on price and differentiates on service, or the way BMW wins on product and is better than most on service. This enables them to have the best margins in their industries. But even these companies are few in number, and nobody can afford to dominate in more than one area. (Then again, maybe differentiating on service in the airlines and automotive industries isn't that difficult.)

LIKE-MINDED PEOPLE

As great teams in business and sports build on their strengths and continue to win, they become known for these strengths. This evolves into their personalities and traditions. It enables them to attract and develop the best people who share the same traits and skills. They win by extending their strengths and doing just enough to solve their weaknesses.

Knowing your strengths and building on them will help you engage people because you'll attract like-minded people who want to do business your way. You'll also develop people in the areas they care about the most. Do just enough to plug your weaknesses, but don't dwell on them, unless they're in your core area or threaten your ability to compete. At the same time, remember the intelligence, skills, attitudes, and values you need reside in a diverse population of people. It's easy to mistake like-minded for "just like me." This can be fatal because you'll choke off the differences that lead to creativity and customer responsiveness.

The St. Louis Cardinals know what kind of talent they want and get it. For as long as they have played in Busch Stadium, the Cardinals have won when they've had great pitching and defense and just enough hitting. Their stars have been their pitchers and fielders, like Bob Gibson, Lou Brock, and Ozzie Smith. They often seem to win with less offense than other teams—usually just a couple of big hitters in the lineup—because their pitching, defense, and speed carry them.

The Cardinals tried to change a few years ago. First, they moved in the outfield fences to encourage more home runs. Then they acquired Mark McGwire, the great home run hitter. But this didn't work; it wasn't true to who the Cardinals were. Even in 1998, when McGwire became the first man to hit 70 home runs in a season, the Cardinals finished third in their division for lack of pitching. The next year, he hit 65 home runs, still a prodigious number, but the Cardinals finished fourth. When this happened, general manager Walt Jocketty and manager Tony LaRussa knew they needed to get back to the Cardinals' traditional strengths of pitching and defense.

Before the 2000 season, Jocketty acquired several veteran starting pitchers, all proven winners. He bolstered the bullpen with a new closer, and improved the defense with second baseman Fernando Vina and center fielder Jim Edmonds. The plan worked beautifully. Although McGwire missed most of the season with injuries, the Cards won their division by a large margin and made the playoffs for the first time since 1996.

The Cardinals kept the same plan for 2001. Looking ahead to the season, Jocketty said, "One thing I would like to improve on for next year is more team speed. We also need to continue to improve our bullpen."[5] No more chasing after big boppers to try and change the Cardinal tradition. In fact, the first trade the Cardinals made for 2001 was to send a power hitting third baseman and a pitching prospect to the Montreal Expos for two quality pitchers.

Despite these acquisitions, the Cardinals struggled until late in the 2001 season. Then, right before the trade deadline, they sent an outfielder to San Diego for pitcher Woody Williams. Williams, a pretty ordinary pitcher, was transformed in St. Louis, and, in turn, changed the Cardinals. When he got there, Williams made some adjustments with the pitching coach and went 7–1 to finish the season and lift the team into the playoffs. The team stayed on its traditional path for 2002 and won its division.

Contrast this with a team that hasn't established a tradition. The NFL's Arizona Cardinals, who used to play in St. Louis, never have established a reputation as being strong at any aspect of the game—passing, running, defense, or special teams. They usually have losing seasons, so they get their share of high draft choices. Still, ownership and management have been too impatient or inept to point the team in a consistent direction. They haven't created strengths to build on, so they haven't prospered.

Most losing teams—in sports or business—don't know who they are or get away from what made them successful. When that occurs, any kind of talent will do, but it usually doesn't mesh into a coherent whole. It doesn't matter whether you're a driver or a builder. Both kinds of leaders make these mistakes and don't engage people in a consistent direction. Whatever talent these teams have usually dissipates because people don't pull together or build on each other.

SELECT FOR FIT

During the three years I worked on gathering data for *Fortune*'s list of the 100 best companies to work for, we asked organizations how they hired people. The top companies always told us selection for fit with their values and beliefs was the most important criterion they used. This meant looking at how new hires would fit in with the company's culture, people, and operating style, not just whether they would get the job done. If someone didn't fit with the team and couldn't do the job the way the organization wanted it done, he or she wouldn't be hired. This puts a premium on people's values, enthusiasm, teamwork abilities, and interpersonal skills.

What separated the best from the rest was how careful the best were in selecting new employees for cultural fit. The best spent significantly more time, money, and effort to pick the best employees who fit. Other companies didn't put the same resources into it or were content just to find people who had the technical skills to do the job. An amazing number of companies think fitting a person to the job requirements is enough, but the best employers understand each hire is a strategic move. Your work culture must sync with your strategy, so your hires must fit your culture.

I see a few differences between builders and drivers in selecting for fit. Some builders give people more latitude—both in whom they select and in feeling they can persuade people to change and fit. Phil Jackson and Dennis Green will do this. They succeed with

some people and not with others. Drivers tend to have very defini-
tive views of who they want—people who will follow their plans.
This often works right away, but drivers tend to not look as closely
at values and behaviors. This is one reason drivers often fail in the
long term. They're also more likely to have less ambitious selection
criteria and a greater willingness to get rid of people who don't
produce in the short term.

Should you pick people who only fit with your style? Absolutely not. You need the complementary styles on your team to balance things and build a winning chemistry. A team of only drivers
will fight each other over goals and who's in charge. A team of only
builders will struggle over process and fall short on accountability.

I experienced this with an executive team I worked with in the
financial industry. It was all builders except for one driver whose
position was not in the core functions of the business so his influence was limited. Most of the builders assumed that all employees
were good people, there to do right for the company and customers.
As a result, for a long time they resisted acting on a few really nasty
and selfish employees, people who disrupted the work in their departments, complained all the time, and provided service based on
their moods, not the customers' needs. This crummy behavior ruined the morale of people around them and discouraged coworkers
who wanted to do well. Why bother to perform if leadership allowed this to continue? Meanwhile, when confronted about this,
executives responded that coaching would correct the problem. Unfortunately, they had let things slide for too long—the situation was
much too ugly for that. With a lot of education, we got the right
leaders to confront the disrupters with the choice to either change
or leave. The ensuing changes and departures raised the mood and
service throughout the whole company.

Should you pick people you like? Absolutely. There's nothing worse than having someone on your team you can't stand. It raises the tension level for you, the person you don't like, and everyone else on the team. If you don't like a person, everyone will know it and others probably won't like him either. Dick Vermeil says that the "l" in leadership is for likeability.[6] You need to like the people on your team.

Obviously it's hard to care for someone you don't like or to build a positive relationship with that person. One caveat: don't be narrow in your tastes about people. That leads to discriminatory behavior. Likeability doesn't have anything to do with race, gender, religion, or other background issues. If it does for you, get over it. Learn to like a wide variety of people. You'll become a better person.

The Oakland A's have selection for fit figured out. The A's never have much money to spend. The team had the fifth lowest payroll in the American League on opening day 2000, second lowest in baseball in 2001, and third lowest in 2002. Still, they won the AL West Division Championship in 2000 and made the playoffs in 2001 and 2002 by sticking to a formula for fit. The formula is based on general manager Billy Beane's belief, "You can get a good bat for 20 cents on the dollar. Pitching's going to cost you two dollars on the dollar."[7] The A's don't have much money, so they spend it very wisely.

Beane and the A's focus on young power hitting because it fits their niche strategy. It's cheap and this is the one thing they do best, so they build on their strength. They also draft pitchers out of college, who can become stars before they get too expensive. Here's their formula.

- No high-priced free agents

- Draft power hitters out of high school

- Teach hitters to take pitches and draw walks in the minor leagues; rewards are given for players who walk a lot and those who don't are traded or released (walks are important because they put people on base in front of the power hitters and wear out opposing pitchers)

- Draft pitchers out of college because they'll reach the big leagues sooner

- Bring in a few low-priced veterans to act as "mentors" to the young players

- Invest in a baseball academy in the Dominican Republic to find cheap talent

- Fill in the gaps by trading for or signing unwanted players and not surrendering much player value or money in return

Pat Gillick, general manager of the Mariners described Beane and his formula this way: "He doesn't detract from his game plan. He has a certain profile of the player he's looking for and certain parameters he has to work under."[8]

Beane and his assistants also are known to take risks and make a big trade if they can. "They're prepared," Rockies general manager Dan O'Dowd says. "They know what they want to do. They're not afraid to make a decision. If they really want to get something done, they make it work."[9]

If the A's can hang onto enough good young pitchers before they leave for more money in free agency, this approach has a chance to take them all the way to the top. It should, at least, help them be competitive and profitable most years against teams with much greater resources. Like the A's, *you must have a detailed approach to selection for fit.* You have to articulate the characteristics you want that go far beyond whether someone can do the job. They must include personal characteristics that fit with what you believe and how you do business. Then go after the best people you can. Successful leaders and companies always spend more time and money on the process of hiring the best. When talent determines whether you win or lose, your return on investment goes up when you put more effort into getting better people.

Even when money's no object, smart teams look for fit. At the end of every season, the Yankees evaluate their talent to decide what free agents to pursue to contend for another World Championship. "Whoever we bring in here will have to fit," said general manager Brian Cashman,[10] who knows Joe Torre won't accept it any other way. Cashman learned this in 2000 when he acquired slugger Jose Canseco for the pennant drive although Torre didn't want him. Torre ended up leaving Canseco off the postseason roster.

At the same time, *in a free agent world, free agents get to choose too.* Mike Mussina had his pick of several teams to play for in 2001 and expressed a desire to play in a smaller town closer to his home in central Pennsylvania. One of the factors that helped him select the Yankees was that Joe Torre called him right after the World Series to tell him how much he wanted him on the team. Other Yankee players called also to tell him he could live a quiet life in the suburbs, much like he had in Baltimore. Mussina said this show of appreciation made a huge difference in deciding where to sign.[11]

Fit also was crucial when all-pro quarterback Rich Gannon signed with the Oakland Raiders. Gannon had played for the Raiders' despised rivals, the Kansas City Chiefs, hated the Oakland team, and thought it lacked discipline. But then-Raiders coach Jon Gruden studied Gannon carefully and decided he was his man because of his work ethic, intensity, abilities to run a complex offense, and decision making on the field. Both are hard-driving people, so Gruden thought they could be terrific together.

Gruden's task was to convince Gannon he could help him bring greater discipline to the Raiders. He appealed to Gannon's work ethic and businesslike approach to the game. At their first meeting, they went out for a quick, cheap meal and headed right to Gruden's office to study film. Gannon said, "I knew right then [this was the right place]." Gruden's instincts were confirmed. "I felt we clicked right away. I had never been around a guy so passionate about playing."[12] Gannon led the Raiders to the AFC Championship game in 2000, losing to the eventual Super Bowl champion Ravens. He led them deep into the playoffs again in 2001, before losing to the soon-to-be-champion Patriots on a snowy night in Massachusetts.

Bill Walsh, who led the San Francisco 49ers to three Super Bowl championships and then helped rebuild the team as general manager ten years later, never abandoned his philosophy of how to build great football teams. Like most professional football people, Walsh knows a strong defense and solid running game form the foundation to winning. What's unique is his approach to talent. Walsh feels offense can be taught, but defense comes from the genes.

According to Walsh, "The only way you can play defense is with athletes. Offensively you can coach a system of football that can be productive, but defensively you have to have players."[13] This means using high draft choices or free agent dollars to get the best athletes available for defense and using what's left on offense.

The keys to good selection for fit are knowing what you're looking for and having an experienced, first-class hiring department. Brian Sabean of the San Francisco Giants thinks the secret is knowledge. "Our emphasis is on experience. In the front office, in scouting, and player development, we have personnel with, on average, 20-plus years in the game."[14]

This is the same approach the Vikings took under Dennis Green and continue under new coach Mike Tice, and they develop good new players every year. Green loved offensive talent and for years relied on a veteran group of five front office people who had been together a long time—more than 90 years of experience with the Vikings among them. Near the end of his Viking career, some people said Green stopped listening to this group, and this contributed to his downfall. All of these men survived Green's departure; in fact, many of them got bigger responsibilities.[15]

Perennial losers like the Cincinnati Bengals illustrate what happens when you underinvest in selection. The team hasn't made the playoffs for more than ten years, the longest drought of any NFL team. Despite the high draft picks the team gets almost every year, it hasn't had a winning record since 1990.

The Bengals have front office and scouting problems. Mike Brown, the owner, is his own president and general manager. He refuses to hire a personnel professional or give power over personnel decisions to his coach. Most successful football teams take one of those two approaches. He also employs one of the smallest scouting staffs in the league, only five full-timers, when many teams have twice that. Brown denies these are the reasons the Bengals are so bad, but the abysmal record is there for everyone to see, especially the deprived fans, many of whom wear bags over their heads at games for fear they'll be recognized. Some players criticize the team so often Brown had to put a clause in contracts to prevent them from slamming the Bengals in public.[16]

When companies ask me what is the most strategically important people practice, I always answer "selection for fit." If you get that right, everything else about leading people to high performance can fall into place. In particular, you'll build the kind of culture you want, and this will unleash your talent to achieve great things.

To do this well, you have to be very detailed about the types of people you want to hire, particularly regarding values, attitudes, and how they work together, and you have to overinvest in evaluating people for hire and promotion. There's no substitute for creating deep expertise in selection.

FIT VERSUS TALENT

What happens when someone of great talent doesn't fit within your company? Sports teams, particularly in pro basketball, are famous for chasing talent and not worrying about fit. Maybe it's because the teams are smaller, so coaches think they can make misfits conform. However, because the team is smaller, every player has more impact to help or hinder victory. Beware of this if you are leading a small work group—one bad apple will ruin your whole bunch.

Leaders, both builders and drivers, often feel they can tame anyone. This isn't a difference of style, it's the difference between a big ego and a strong ego. Big egos often overestimate what they're capable of doing. Some of the merger mania in business comes from executives believing they should be running bigger companies while lacking the patience and discipline to grow them organically. Big egos ignore or discount the substantial data that shows that most mergers fail; big egos are sure they can make them work.

Sometimes taking on a questionable person works, but only with a lot of help and great pain. Many times it's a disaster. Phil Jackson took on bad boy Dennis Rodman with the Bulls because he desperately needed a rebounder. Rodman helped the Bulls win three NBA titles, despite constant acting out. But Jackson wasn't the only one trying to contain Rodman. Michael Jordan laid down the law too, and he had a big influence on Rodman who knew better than to mess with Michael.

It didn't work out so well in Los Angeles for Jackson with J.R. Rider. Jackson took on Rider, a notorious troublemaker for coaches and teammates, because the Lakers needed another offensive weapon. The coach figured he could tame him like he did Rodman. However, Rider disrupted the team; Jackson called this "The Rider Effect."[17] In L.A., neither Shaquille O'Neal nor Kobe Bryant were mature enough to play the Jordan role with Rider. The best Jackson could do was to bury Rider at the end of the bench so he wasn't a big distraction.

Maybe the longest ongoing feud in basketball is between Philadelphia 76ers' coach Larry Brown and his star, Allen Iverson. Iverson doesn't like Brown's demands and every year Brown threatens to quit or trade Iverson, one of the best players in the NBA. For his part, Iverson said the one word he wanted on his tombstone was "misunderstood," because that's how he feels about the way Brown treats him.[18]

In this case, the rift healed during the 2000–2001 NBA season because Brown, a demanding driver, learned to relax about Iverson's off-the-court behavior and offered more on-the-court praise. Brown showed a versatility that wasn't always there before. For his part, Iverson matured and began to understand what Brown wanted. Both sides changed to make it work, and it did. Brown and Iverson combined to lead the Sixers to the NBA finals against the mighty Lakers. Too bad the wound reopened during the next season.

When talent and fit clash, you have three choices. You can stick to your system and get assistance from peer leadership to help the outlier conform. This is rarely a complete success, but it can work if the person genuinely wants to do well. Builders can make this work better than drivers because they're more likely to foster peer leadership.

Or you can get rid of the person because you think your team will function better without him or her in the long term. This usually is referred to as "addition by subtraction." Your team may actually be less talented, but improvements in focus, teamwork, and chemistry may overcome the loss. Drivers usually are more willing to make this tough call sooner than builders.

Finally, you can relax your methods a bit and hope the person will respond. For a driver, this is a sign of versatility and can lead you to becoming more engaging. To do this, listen more carefully and try to understand the person's needs that he may not be communicating to you, increase your praise to the person when he behaves properly to shape him in the correct direction, and create a more positive atmosphere. If you're right about the person, this'll work.

Be aware, however, that trying to reform a truly bad apple can be dangerous. Letting up on your standards will cause chaos if the person doesn't come around. The others on your team will perceive that your structure has broken down and some of them will act out too. If this happens, you're not a driver or builder who's trying to be more versatile, you're just a leader with a big ego who made a mistake.

Obviously, all of these choices are high risk. Unless you're dealing with an extraordinary talent and have great support from the person's peers, you're probably better off getting rid of the person. How often do people mature when you need them to?

TALENT VERSUS GENIUS

Larry Brown agonized waiting for Allan Iverson to grow up and lead, but he didn't have much choice. Philadelphia didn't have a lot of other talent and had built the team around him. The Sixers breakthrough performance in 2000–2001 probably came just in time to save the team. Otherwise Brown, Iverson, or both would have been gone.

The Lakers already had one star in O'Neal, but they put up with Bryant's egocentric behavior during 2000–2001 for a different reason. Bryant showed flashes of real genius.

This is the one exception to the idea about getting rid of the person who doesn't fit. If the person is a real genius at what he or she does, you have to work with the individual and wait for him or her to mature. You'll also have to change some of the ways you lead. *There isn't much real genius in the world. If you're lucky enough to encounter it, let it flow. It will raise the standards you set for your team.*

There's an old saying, "Genius does what it must, talent does what it can." Could Bryant's stubbornness be a sign of genius? Did his rare gift force him to challenge O'Neal, or was it just ego?

On a small team it's almost impossible to have two stars who want to be "da man." It's totally impossible to have them fight with each other or have one who won't buy into the program. Horace Grant played with Jordan and knew this. "You have to put your ego aside. You can't have two Batmans. You have to have one Batman and one Robin."[19]

If you're fortunate enough to have a genius on your team, give him or her as much freedom as you can. Jackson always treated Jordan differently from the rest. Grant may have forgotten, but he didn't like it. Neither did some of the other Bulls, but they saw where Jordan took them. Center Luc Longley said, "I made a career out of backing MJ."[20] The one thing Jackson insisted on was that Jordan learn to trust his teammates and get them involved so they wouldn't just sit back and watch Michael play. It took Jackson a long time to get this point across to Michael, but he had to be patient. When the lesson finally took, all of the Bulls players became better, and they won six championships.

That's the thing about geniuses; they lift everyone else around them. Tiger Woods has required everyone else on the pro golf tour to improve his game to keep up with him. Phil Mickelson, perhaps the second best golfer in the world, said of Woods, "He seems to create shots at very opportune times, which forces me to perform at that same level or higher."[21] Vijay Singh, winner of two major championships, went further. "I think a lot of guys are in awe of him, totally, to the point that they might feel they're five shots behind him before the tournament even starts. The top guys seem to have more trouble with him . . . they think if they don't beat Tiger, it's the end of the world."[22]

Doc Rivers, coach of the Orlando Magic saw the similarity of Woods's and Jordan's impacts on their competition, "I look at Phil Mickelson and David Duval, and that must be the way Karl Malone, John Stockton, and Patrick Ewing felt throughout their careers. Why did I have to be born now?"[23]

Fortunately for the rest of us, there aren't many geniuses out there. We don't have to feel like we're starting five shots behind. However, you'll end up way behind if you have a genius on your team and don't recognize it.

CHANGE YOUR TALENT OR CHANGE TO YOUR TALENT?

When you don't have the talent you need to play the way you want, you have two choices. You can change your talent, or you can adapt to what you have. *An engaging leader takes the shortest path to victory.* If your talent is wrong or lacking, replace it or add to it. If the talent is there, change your approach to mesh with it.

For several years, CDW Computer Centers has been recognized as the best employer in Illinois. For years, like other best employers, CDW relied on promotion from within. Our Hewitt studies showed that most of the best employers are like Southwest Airlines. To maintain its unique culture, Southwest rarely hired senior people from the outside, always preferring to elevate internal candidates. Founder Michael Krasny did the same in building the unique, dynamic CDW culture—people grew with him as it became a $4 billion enterprise. However, when Krasny was ready to step aside, he knew he needed a different kind of leadership to nurture a more mature organization through slower markets. He hired a chairman and CEO from the outside. The new boss, John Edwardson, brought in other new senior executives to deepen and diversify the executive team, all the while hiring carefully for fit.

When Dick Vermeil took over the St. Louis Rams in 1997, he knew he didn't have enough good talent. "Only nine players from the 1997 team I inherited were good enough to play on my 2000 Super Bowl Champions."[24] When Jim Haslett, another driver, became coach of the New Orleans Saints, he also did a major makeover, but he did it faster.

Haslett and general manager Randy Mueller took over the Saints in 2000 following a 3–13 season in 1999 under Mike Ditka, who had lost his passion for coaching. The Saints had only five winning seasons in 34 years, but the Ditka years were especially painful because of his larger-than-life reputation and the high expectations that accompanied him to New Orleans.

Haslett and Mueller set out to change the entire chemistry of the team. They kept its strength—many of the offensive and defensive linemen—but picked up 31 new players through trades, free agent signings, and the draft, despite not having a first or third round draft pick. Mueller said, "We didn't want people who were hindered by the past failures of the Saints."[25]

The team was plagued by injuries all season. It lost three starters in its first preseason game alone. During the year, the Saints also lost their starting quarterback, running back, and other key players. Through it all, Haslett kept them together. He took an organized but highly competitive approach to coaching. When a player went down, Haslett just turned to the next one in line and told him to step it up. Mueller thinks Haslett is one of a kind, "He just has an innate ability of being able to kick the players in the butt and have them hugging him five minutes later and playing their tails off for him."[26]

The results were miraculous. The Saints went 11–5, won the NFC Western Division title, and knocked off the Rams in the first round of the playoffs. They also discovered a quarterback for the future in Aaron Brooks. No one had heard of Brooks until he took over with six games left in the season and led the team into the playoffs. For his success, Haslett won coach of the year honors.

But Haslett, like a lot of drivers, had trouble sustaining his success. In 2001, he "lost" his team and it collapsed during the last stretch of the season. The Saints seemed to tune Haslett out after he came down hard on one player with discipline problems but let another one off easy. There were other locker room jealousies too. The team stopped playing very hard and missed the playoffs, after being in the running for the early part of the year. After the season, Mueller and Haslett were at it again, making big changes in the roster and coaching staff, adjusting the chemistry and talent levels. Ironically, Mueller made so many changes so fast, the team owner fired him for not keeping him informed of all the details.[27]

Brian Billick, another driver, took the opposite route. Billick was the highly successful offensive coordinator of the Minnesota Vikings when he was hired to lead the Baltimore Ravens in 1999. His 1998 Vikings offense set a record for points scored. Many people regard Billick as something of an offensive genius and a new age thinker. Some others think of him as an egomaniac, a charge to which Billick has pleaded guilty. Previously, he helped Bill Walsh write a book on offense. Billick loves to use the computer to analyze offenses and create new plays. He talks in computer-speak—so much so that his players nicknamed him "Stat Boy." Former Vikings receiver Cris Carter, who played for Billick, said, "I'm kind of a computer guy myself, so a lot of times I understand what he's saying. I speak Billick on occasion."[28]

However, the Ravens team Billick inherited had a tremendous defense and a woeful offense. Rather than a wholesale change of the players on the team, Billick built on what he had. He tried to improve the offense, going through a string of quarterbacks and drafting a running back number one after the 1999 season, but this didn't help much. Mostly, he added to the defense that had been constructed by his terrific defensive coordinator, Marvin Lewis.

The results were outstanding. Despite going five games in October without scoring a touchdown, the Ravens went 15–4 and then won the Super Bowl by shutting down other teams, kicking field goals, and scoring on turnovers. The defense set a record for fewest points allowed in a season, while the offense evolved into a unit that scored just enough points to win while mostly trying to avoid mistakes. "As long as we win, I'll take it," Billick said. "They've pulled me over to the dark side."[29]

In 2001, Billick's Ravens stumbled. They made the playoffs but didn't get very far. Injuries and a bad decision to change quarterbacks by Billick doomed them. Though the team still had a fearsome defense, other teams figured out how to adjust and score on the Ravens, and they encountered the usual problems repeating as champions in the NFL.

They took different approaches, but both Billick and Haslett defined what needed to be done and did it. They weren't afraid to change. Once they identified their strengths, they set their plans accordingly and stuck with them, even when things weren't going well. The Saints' injuries and the Ravens' total inability to score touchdowns didn't stop them. They just kept going, playing to their strengths. No twisting in the wind or pressing the panic button for these two often-engaging drivers.

The lessons for you are clear. First, evaluate what you've got. If it isn't good enough to win, get rid of it. Know what you need and go get it. Second, if your talent is strong, but it doesn't fit your preferred approach, be flexible. Change your ways. Talent is way too valuable to waste because you're stubborn.

The ranks of ex-coaches are full of people who believed in their "system" but didn't have the people who could execute it. His critics in Boston said one of the reasons Rick Pitino failed with the Celtics was because his coaching style that worked so well in college didn't graduate to the pro game. More skilled professional players easily beat the full-court pressure, up-tempo transition, and three-point shooting style of basketball that's his trademark. Pitino wouldn't change, so he went back to coaching college basketball.[30]

TALENT + TOUGHNESS + TEAMWORK = VICTORY

Winning takes talent and mental toughness. Vermeil, Haslett, and Billick all brought a *mental toughness* to their teams that rubbed off on the players and helped them win. Vermeil spent the first two years with the Rams driving the players as hard as he could—extra practices, grueling drills, and endless film sessions—until he could establish the toughness he wanted in his players and see who could handle it. Then he backed off some, knowing that *you can't start out easy and get tougher, but you can start out tough and get easier.* His players asked for and appreciated it.

This is a vital lesson for drivers, who need to know when to ease up, and builders, who need to know when to crack down, so they can become more engaging and successful. Of course, learning how and when to change your style is key. If you don't do it right, it can be your undoing. This is what happened to Haslett, a newer head coach.

Mental toughness means you *expect to win*, believing you're better, stronger, and more resilient than your competitor. You know in your heart you'll find a way to win no matter the obstacles. Communicate this attitude to your team.

Billick likes to talk tough to motivate his players. Before taking his team into archrival Tennessee for a playoff game, he said, "When you go into the lion's den, you don't tippy-toe in. You carry a spear. You go in screaming like a banshee and say, 'Where is the son of a [gun]?' If you go in any other way, you're going to lose."[31] You may not put it in these terms, but you have to instill an expectation of victory in people. People who think they're going to lose, probably will.

A related aspect of mental toughness is putting away your opponent— closing the deal. Michael Jordan was the greatest "closer" in the history of basketball. He wanted the ball in the last minutes so he could take the last shots. He expected to come out on top and used everything at his disposal to do so.

That's another crucial lesson for leaders. *You've got to have a closer*—someone you can turn to when the game or the deal is on the line. You need your own Michael Jordan, an employee whose mental attitude is so tough and his performance is so outstanding that team members know he or she won't let them lose. This might be a project leader who always brings key initiatives in on time and within budget, a department manager who always posts outstanding results, a nurse who sets the tone in the ward and keeps things cool under pressure, or a salesperson who can get the big account. It's your "go to" person. A closer helps you instill toughness in your team. He or she is a big part of the talent you need.

One of the quickest ways to build toughness in sports and business is to form an "us against the world" mentality. Coaches do this all the time—both drivers and builders. Dan Hampton, the hall of fame defensive tackle of the 1985 Super Bowl Chicago Bears, called it "sport's oldest motivational tool."[32] No doubt Mike Ditka used it all the time. Billy Martin, who managed several championship baseball teams, relied on it wherever he went. Billick said he used it during the Ravens' 2000 championship run. He described it as "Going against the odds. You have to take that mentality . . . it's us against the world, even if it's fabricated a little bit."[33] Jackson used it in Chicago, though over time the enemy went from being the Detroit Pistons to the New York Knicks to the Bulls' front office. That's when his reign ended.

There are two weaknesses with this approach that show up much bigger in business than in sports. First, this is a short-term way of doing things. It may last a season, but it won't carry you for the long run. It's basically a "chip on the shoulder" attitude, born of anger. After a while, particularly after some success, it's hard to maintain. Red Auerbach, former general manager and coach of the Boston Celtics who won many times, said the hardest thing to do is to win the second time. The players lose the hunger and they tune out the forced anger. Billick found this out when the Ravens stumbled the year after winning the Super Bowl. Maybe it's why Billy Martin kept changing teams. Business is all about long-run success, so avoid this approach.

Second, though this is an easy way to build your team, it makes it much harder to integrate your team with other teams in your company. This leads to internal competition and destroys larger organizations where processes have to flow across departments. If you start with this approach, how do you change your message so your team will cooperate with other groups whom you taught it to dislike? One company I worked with had so much internal competition it had to develop an evaluation criterion for its leaders that said they could only speak well of other departments.

The right approach for the long term is to set your goal, establish a framework of roles and responsibilities that complement each other, communicate this structure clearly, and then address individual motivations. Michael Jordan put it in these terms, "Talent wins games, but teamwork and intelligence wins championships."[34]

Joe Torre's Yankees took this path. Yes, the team was blessed with fabulous players, but not a single Yankee won the most valuable player or Cy Young award in the team's 1996, 1998, 1999, or 2000 title seasons. Instead, the team got contributions from everyone on its roster, including players who were unknown outside of New York, like Scott Brosius and Luis Sojo. Even star players put the team goal of winning the World Series ahead of their own glory and played whatever roles were asked of them. In particular, they played some of the best team defense anyone had seen in baseball. They knew their rewards would come with victory.

Along the way, Torre built an incredibly mentally tough team. This showed itself in the 2001 playoffs and World Series. Down 2–0 in a five game series to the hottest team in baseball, the Oakland A's, Torre donned his "It ain't over till it's over" hat he got from Yogi Berra and focused the Yanks on winning one game at a time. They did. They beat Oakland three straight times, including twice in Oakland, to win the series.[35]

Nobody needed toughness, teamwork, and intelligence more than the Portland Trail Blazers in the 2000 NBA Western Conference finals. When they played the Lakers in game seven, the team that lost would be done for the season. The Lakers had Kobe and Shaq, both closers in their own ways, and Phil Jackson's inside-out triangle offensive system. The Blazers were a team full of great players, all playing relatively equal roles. As good as they were, no one on the Blazers really was used to carrying a team, of closing things in the last few minutes, and they lacked a coherent way to play together. Their best-known player, Scottie Pippen, was voted one of the NBA's top 50 players of all time, but he made his reputation as Jordan's sidekick.

Portland built a huge second half lead and started the fourth quarter ahead by 16 points. Then the Lakers turned up the pressure and came after them. Nobody on Portland appeared to want the ball. They kept passing up shots, waiting for their teammates to shoot. Meanwhile Kobe and Shaq, with their supporting cast, stepped forward and led a huge rally to win by five points and eliminate the Blazers. It was the most dramatic comeback in NBA playoff history and a great example of talent, toughness, and teamwork.

I ended the first two chapters with questions to help you discover more about your leadership style and your employees. For the rest of the book, I'll give you some tips on how to become a more engaging leader based on the topics in each chapter.

THE HUDDLE

If you're a builder:

- Recognize the strengths of your organization and spend your time building on them. Address your weaknesses quickly if they're crippling your core operations. In particular, focus on your value proposition and what kinds of people you should hire to help you meet it.

- Hire people you like, and people who think like you about your business. But remember to hire people with diverse characteristics—don't hire only other builders.

- Select people who not only have the technical skills for the job, but also fit into your organization. Don't give too much latitude to people who don't fit. When in doubt, throw them out.

- Don't think you can change people. Be quicker to let go the ones who don't fit. You can more easily bring in new people that fit than reform the current ones that don't.

- Communicate more toughness and raise your standards, particularly in the face of business challenges.

If you're a driver:

- Recognize the strengths of your organization and spend your time building on them. Don't be stubborn about fixing weaknesses unless they're crippling. In particular, focus on your value proposition and what kinds of people you should hire to help you meet it.

- Hire people you like, and people who think like you about your business. But remember to hire people with diverse characteristics—don't hire only other drivers.

- Select people who not only have the technical skills for the job, but also fit into your organization. Be sure to look at their values and behaviors—how they get results—not only at their ability to deliver results.

- Recognize when you have to change your approach to match your people. Don't be too quick to judge or get rid of team

members. Develop some peer leaders to help you bring people together.

- Communicate high standards and mental toughness but know when to back off and relax a little.

TALENT

Develop and Diversify

"There's no I in team, *but there is in* win."

—Michael Jordan[1]

THE RETURN OF THE INDIVIDUAL

Former baseball manager Billy Martin said he had one set of rules, but he applied them 25 different ways. This was his way of recognizing and respecting each player as an individual. Billy understood this because he was an eccentric individual himself. Billy Martin was ahead of his time.

When I did MBA recruiting at Hewitt Associates, the audience always started the question-and-answer part of the meeting with the same two questions: What are you going to do to develop me? and What do you do about work-life balance? *Development and balance are on people's minds* today—not just on the minds of MBA students. National surveys tell us these two concerns are foremost for all employees.

Rather than answer myself, I asked each individual on our recruiting team to talk about his or her own situation. This was much

more powerful than reciting our policies or rattling off facts and fig-
ures. The audience could hear how others felt about how they were
developing at the firm and understand that each individual was
free to work out his or her own accommodations within the needs
of our business.

Then, typically, I would get a third question: "How do you
show that you value *diversity*?" This was something we were trying
to improve as a management team, so I took this issue myself.

Hewitt did a good job on development and balance, but we fell
short on diversity. Our hearts were in the right place, but we had
trouble implementing plans and needed to get much better. But we
didn't work hard at any of these things to be nice. We did them to
get and keep the talent that was the life source of our company.
These issues engage people. *To become an engaging leader, you have to
pay attention to development, balance, and diversity.*

When people ask you about these things, they're really questioning whether and how you're going to help them build their
skills and live their lives. They want you to do this in ways that
show you'll recognize, reward, and respect them as individuals. In
essence, they are asking, "Are you going to value and help me grow
as a unique individual, or do you want me to be like everyone
else?" If you want them to be like everyone else, you won't attract
much talent when skilled people are in short supply.

Some leaders, both drivers and builders, preach teamwork
above everything else, but it's hitting the right blend between teamwork and individualism that counts now. Increasingly, this favors
the individual. Talent becomes more mobile every year, and teams
aren't free agents; individuals are.

Brian Billick's players felt he let them be themselves on the road
to the Super Bowl. Then Ravens' defensive end Rob Burnett said,
"He doesn't want a team made from cookie-cutters, he wants us all

to be individuals."[2] This led to a lot of barking and bragging on the way to winning the big game. The media criticized Billick and the team for it, but they didn't care. Popularity with sportswriters wasn't going to help them win.

Providing strong development opportunities enables you to get and keep talent while you're building the workforce skills you need. Ensuring people can have balanced lives will help you get the most out of people because they'll appreciate what you're doing for them. They'll stay for the long run. Valuing diversity means you'll get the broadest array of talent possible and be better able to serve a wide range of customers. Addressing all three issues—development, balance, and diversity—with total zeal will help you build your dynasty.

BUILD A DYNASTY

You create a dynasty by building leadership and talent year after year to keep winning. Becoming a dynasty should be your long-term goal. There have been a few dynasties in pro sports—the Montreal Canadiens, Celtics, Lakers, Bulls, Green Bay Packers, Dallas Cowboys, Pittsburgh Steelers, 49ers, and the greatest dynasty of all, the Yankees. It's become much harder to win consistently in recent years with free agency. That's why the Yankees' record over the last several years is so remarkable.

Business dynasties have had it easier until recently. When loyalty reigned and there were more people than jobs, people stayed with their companies. Continuity of talented people could contribute to keeping you on top because those people knew how to get things done in your company and how to serve your customers. You also could grow your leaders from within, and that encouraged people about their own opportunities.

That has changed. Even the best companies now turn over the equivalent of their entire workforces every five or six years. CEO turnover among the largest U.S. companies runs about 20 to 25 percent per year, with about 15 percent of the new leaders coming from outside the company.[3]

Yet the formula for building dynasties is pretty clear for both sports and business. *Start by creating a strong foundation of talent from within.* In business, this occurs through good selection and development. In sports, it's the same, selecting through good drafting and developing through the farm system and other ways. Grow these people and evaluate which ones are the keepers. Get rid of the rest, then fill in your gaps with free agents. That's how the Yankees, Braves, Packers, Lakers, and other teams that win year after year do it.

Hockey is full of free agents who jump teams every year, but the teams closest to dynasties now are the Colorado Avalanche and the New Jersey Devils. They take pride in homegrown talent, with a few key free agents added as needed. From 1995 to 2002, Colorado won eight straight division titles and two Stanley Cups. The Devils won four division titles and two Cups. They played each other for the 2001 Stanley Cup, with Colorado winning. The Avs had 11 draft picks on the 2001 championship team that beat the Devils, who played with nine draft picks. In the 2002 playoffs, they each lost to a team that made it to the finals, including the champion Red Wings.

Lou Lamoriello, the Devils' general manager, says the key to success is developing a philosophy for drafting talent. His view of selecting young players starts with the heart. "There's such a thing as a Devils' player. He can be of any style, but he has to have something here [in his heart] that we can't teach. The core of the players and veterans will not accept anything other than the best out of each other."[4] Then the Devils trade as needed to bring in new players.

The other two strategies—only grow from within or buy all your talent—aren't viable for most companies, though a few very special places, like Southwest Airlines and Harley Davidson, appear to grow almost everybody. You probably can't grow fast enough if you only make all your own talent, nor can you compete continually with organizations that are able to bring in key free agents. Some of your young talent just won't develop or stay with you. Eventually, you'll have a skill gap you can't fill from inside and another company will pass you by. The more highly skilled jobs you have, the truer this is.

On the other hand, if you continually go to the outside for most of your talent, you rarely get the chemistry, trust, and communication you need. I once consulted to an oil company that was unusual in the industry because it was made up largely of executives from the outside. One vice president said to me, "We've got great people, but we've got no culture." This prevented them from sharing knowledge because there wasn't enough commonality among the people, their values, and the ways they were used to doing business.

As Seattle pitcher Norm Charlton said, "The one thing about signing free agents is you never know what you're going to get, attitudewise."[5] When a majority of key people are outsiders, they may look out for themselves more than for your goals. Enron had a huge number of outsiders. We've seen this in recent years with teams like the Boston Red Sox, Los Angeles Dodgers, and Texas Rangers. They spend a fortune but keep turning over players and rarely win. Wholesale changes only work when there's a disaster.

The crucial skill that makes or breaks your opportunity to create a dynasty is your ability to evaluate talent. You must know whom to select and develop and whom to avoid or let go. Evaluation of people is the toughest thing a leader does; it's the hardest skill to master. It's particularly difficult when you have good relationships with your

people. Still, engaging leaders have to do it. This is the same philosophy Jack Welch used at General Electric where he insisted on
rigorous performance evaluation, including generously rewarding
the top 20 percent of performers and firing the bottom 10 percent
every year.

Dick Vermeil says *honesty is the key to good evaluation*, "If you're
always honest with them [the players], and you have the right communications system going, they understand because you've never
misled them. They always know the bottom line is the bottom line."[6]

You also have to be honest with yourself. Lamoriello says you
have to admit your mistakes in selection and do it quickly. You can't
wait several years to see if someone will make it. "When we make
a mistake, we hold our hand up. The bottom line is to get the best
players out there to play. If they're not, move on. As soon as you
know they're not, get rid of them before somebody else finds out
they're not."[7]

Drivers and builders bring different strengths to these issues.
Builders are oriented toward developing people for long-term success, which is a characteristic of a dynasty. In fact, I think builders
often follow the old Chinese proverb for dynasty creation.

> If you want 1 year of prosperity, grow grain.
> If you want 10 years of prosperity, grow trees.
> If you want 100 years of prosperity, grow people.

Drivers will make a tough call on talent and performance
sooner, which is necessary to weed out poor performers. They'll
turn people over faster. This means they often hire more experienced people. GE and PepsiCo, companies built on a hard-driving
model, traditionally hire and fire more senior people than many
other companies.

Still, to build a dynasty that engages people for sustained success, you need to both develop and evaluate.

THE DEVELOPMENT MANDATE

If you're going to build a dynasty, you have no choice but to start by growing as much talent as you can. That's your mandate for development. Today, more than ever, your highly skilled employees demand it. In fact, if you don't focus on the individual development needs of your high-flying young talents, you shouldn't even bother to recruit them. They'll leave in a few years.

In a recent survey of high-potential gen X managers and executives at global companies, a majority of people said they had no developmental contracts or plans. Almost half said their companies invested little or nothing in their personal development. As a result, 40 percent said they planned on leaving within two years.[8] Those companies are wasting that talent.

That's another thing I found when I helped collect data for *Fortune*'s 100 best places to work list. Great employers offered more hours of training to their employees every year. They offered more approaches to growing people so development plans could be as unique as the people pursuing them. They also put a heavy emphasis on promotion from within. These companies retained their talent much better than others who didn't emphasize development as heavily.

Again, the Super Bowl champion Ravens prove the point. Nine of the 11 players they've drafted in the first two rounds since 1995 were starters. It's only when you need to do a complete makeover, like the New Orleans Saints, that you should put free agents and newcomers above development.

What happens if you don't develop people? You don't win. Four of the worst teams in baseball in 2002 were the Milwaukee Brewers, Chicago Cubs, Tampa Bay Devil Rays and Baltimore Orioles. None of these teams had all-star players on their rosters whom they drafted and developed. Meanwhile, five of the Yankees' six all-stars were homegrown talents.

You also need to know whom to develop. While great employers offer a large menu of learning opportunities to everyone, smart leaders pick out their best and brightest to help them grow into future leaders. They determine who should receive special and accelerated opportunities. They know everyone can be taught leadership but not everyone can learn it. Focus significant time and attention on those with the most potential. Above all, let them know you're doing it. This will increase their motivation to stay. People want to feel special.

A really interesting story is happening in basketball with the Los Angeles Clippers, of all teams. The Clippers may be the most pathetic franchise in the history of the NBA. In 18 seasons in Los Angeles, the team has had one winning record. It never seemed to have a plan, careening from building with youth to chasing free agents or trading for veterans of questionable talent. The only constant in the team's strategy was doing things cheaply. Because it always lost, it always had high draft choices. But with the lack of direction, terrible records, constant turnover of coaches, and an owner who wouldn't pay to keep them, young stars couldn't wait to get away as soon as they could.

Then, after the 1999–2000 season, buoyed by a new arena, the team made an all-out commitment to building with youth. It made deals to acquire two additional first round draft choices to add to the one it already had. One of the deals also brought a 1999 first rounder from another team. This enabled it to add four great young players to some skilled, high draft choices from the prior years. All of a sudden, the Clippers had some great young talent.

Just as important as acquiring the talent was the selection of players and the team's commitment to their development. Three of the newcomers—Quentin Richardson, Corey Maggette and Darius Miles—were high school friends from Illinois. These three knew they could rely on each other to make the transition to pro basketball. They each brought family members out to live with them to be their support systems.[9] The teammates and their families socialized together to keep from being homesick. The team also brought in a new coach, Alvin Gentry, who had a reputation as a teacher and a builder, and he supplemented his staff with other coaches who could teach. Finally, the team sprinkled in a few veterans to help show the younger players how to manage in the NBA.

The first year results were great. The Clippers won more games midway through the 2000–2001 season than they had in any of their three previous seasons. Attendance at games was way up, and they were finally able to beat their crosstown rivals, the Lakers, once in a while.

With the core in place, the Clippers switched to phase two: trading for some young, but more experienced players. Their big deal before the 2001–2002 season was to get Elton Brand, a two-year veteran with real leadership abilities. They acquired Brand from the Bulls for a draft pick, instead of using the pick to choose another high school player or someone with only a year of college. Brand is a role model of steadiness and strong work ethic, as well as a talented player who made the all-star team. The Clippers still had a losing record in 2001–2002, but won more games than it had in years, almost making the playoffs. Of course, the real payoff will come only if the Clippers keep these players together for the long term. If the team is willing to spend the money to do that, it could end its long-running misery.

Pick the right people and have plans and support mechanisms in place to develop them. Tailor development strategies and tactics to each individual. Identify what people need to learn to perform at higher levels, put them in positions where they can succeed if they stretch, and then push them hard to develop them. Kraft Foods calls this "leaning into people." It's part of their developmental philosophy, and it has created more talent for itself and more CEOs for other companies than any other organization I can think of, with the possible exception of GE, which is several times larger. When you develop people and reward their successes the right ways, you can lean into them all the way to the top.

CLOSE YOUR GAPS

With a solid core of skilled talent, you can fill in your talent gaps with free agents. Before you do this, be certain that there are no internal candidates. Then go outside for what you need.

With this kind of hiring, it's critical to do two things. First, make sure the person fits your hiring profile, especially matching your values and beliefs. This likely will take a long interviewing process, much more exhaustive than you might be used to doing. Next, communicate to your existing staff why it is important to go outside. Your people will want to know this isn't a change from your primary emphasis on growing from within and there still will be opportunities available for them. When CDW went outside for its new leader, it had to tell people why—in this case the heir apparents weren't quite ready—and reaffirm its belief in developing from within.

In business, you have to buy what you don't have, but in sports you can fill in your gaps with free agents or trades. Developing a core of good young talent is even more valuable because it saves you money. This brings us back to evaluating talent. Brian Sabean knows this. "The real key is to decide the right guys to trade. You want to hold on to the golden nuggets."[10]

The Yankees are the masters at this. The widespread perception is they built their championship teams by buying free agents. In reality, the core of the talent is homegrown—Bernie Williams, Derek Jeter, Andy Pettite, Romero Mendoza, Mariano Rivera, and Jorge Posada—or acquired in trades for other players, like Roger Clemons, Chuck Knoblauch, and Paul O'Neill. In mid-summer 2000, the Yankees traded prospects to acquire David Justice, Denny Neagle, and Glenallen Hill for the stretch run. In 2001 and 2002, they traded prospects for pitchers.

One reason people believe the Yankees rely so much on free agents is that most of the prospects they trade don't develop. In essence, it seems like they get something for nothing. They often do, but it's not from just buying talent. More importantly, they get rid of people who aren't going to be very good before the other teams find out—just what Lamoriello said. New York lets very few good players get away; Jay Buhner of Seattle and Eric Milton and Christian Guzman of Minnesota come to mind as the only players who left the Yankees through trades and became stars. Ted Lilly may be another.

More often you have to give talent to get talent. The St. Louis Cardinals' trade of a top prospect led to success in their 2000 season and beyond. They knew they had a very good team, but identified a gap in outfield defense and hitting. The team traded away a great infield prospect, Adam Kennedy, and a veteran pitcher to get Jim Edmonds from the Anaheim Angels. Kennedy became a very special player for the Angels, and Edmonds was terrific for St. Louis in 2000. He was the Cards' most valuable player, hitting .295 with 42 home runs and 108 runs batted in, and playing superb centerfield. He even hit the home run that beat Atlanta in the first round of the NL playoffs. He had great seasons in 2001 and 2002 also. The Cardinals' surplus of young talent made this possible.

Here's where business has an advantage over sports. You don't have to give up talent to get more. Just keep adding to what you have. In sports, it's possible to have too many players fighting for the same position. But engaging business leaders know they can never have enough talent because expanding talent pools will expand their companies. Meanwhile, all the other rules of building dynasties are the same. Select the right people for the right reasons, evaluate your talent honestly, invest in developing people, and fill in your gaps with experienced hires that fit. This is your recipe for success.

DIFFERENT STROKES

As an engaging leader, you face a paradox. People are more self-reliant these days and more skeptical of organizations, withholding loyalty because they don't believe it will be returned. At the same time, you need more from your people, and they need more from you. You demand more hours and results. They need more resources from you to help manage their lives, families, even their pets. A recent survey of American workers reported that 88 percent said the struggle to balance their work and personal lives was their biggest issue.[11] Because every person's situation is different, you can't have a "one size fits all" answer. You have to tailor your responses to each person.

That's why issues about balance and diversity are merging. A few smart companies have recognized this, but most haven't, though they must. *Balance and diversity are both about respecting individuals.*

Moreover, taking an integrated view of balance and diversity pays off in retaining talent. For example, research done by Professor George Dreher of Indiana University shows that companies that offer more work-life benefits are better able to keep and grow female middle managers and senior executives. These family-friendly employers create programs and policies that enable women to juggle their careers and roles as mothers.[12]

In general, this is one place where builders have an advantage over drivers. Their greater tolerance for individual differences makes them naturally more comfortable with these issues. However, drivers can stand out as versatile and engaging leaders by embracing balance and diversity. They can bring their tremendous energy to these areas and really make a difference for their people. Regardless of style, *your challenge is to celebrate all your people for the different gifts they bring—no matter where they came from or how they got there—and help them use their gifts to advance your goals.* This is a huge test, but it's how you engage people for high performance. It took Larry Brown years, yet he finally passed it.

Brown, coach of the Philadelphia 76ers, and his star, Allen Iverson, battled for years because of their differences. Brown's a highly driven member of the Ike generation—placing team and duty first. Iverson is a poster child for gen X in the NBA. Self and personal experience come first. Their feud even led to threats of trading Iverson, a ridiculous idea because the team was built around him.

According to Brown, "I've always felt that in his own way, Allen was trying to win games. My issues have been off the court." For his part, Iverson pointed out, "When I first came into the league, everybody saw the talent God gave me and wanted to make me a guy who was 35 years old. Nobody ever gave me room for mistakes."[13]

Iverson played brilliantly in 2000–2001, leading the Sixers to the NBA finals and winning the MVP award, amazing for one of the shortest players in the league. But he and Brown fought for most of the first half of the season. Brown even took a short break away from the team due to the stress. Iverson made headlines with his troubles. He released a rap album with lyrics offensive to women and gay people, swore at a fan in the stands, and showed up late for practices early in the year. Finally, he and Brown reached a truce. It occurred when Brown started listening to Iverson and gave him the freedom and praise he needed, and Iverson told Brown he wanted to have a strong relationship with him. As Brown said, "I still don't like his music or the way he dresses, but Allen has a lot of good in him, and I'm finding it out every single day."[14]

To engage a wide spectrum of people, you have to learn the same lessons Larry Brown did. Focus on the performance that comes from diverse people, not their differences. Create more opportunities for understanding and valuing the unique qualities of people different from you.

MORE DIVERSITY MEANS MORE TALENT

September 10, 2000, was something of a red-letter day for diversity in sports.

- There were 14 NFL games. The starting quarterbacks in those games included nine African-Americans, one Hispanic, and one Jew.

- A black woman, Venus Williams, and a 20-year-old Russian male, Marat Safin, won the U.S. Open in tennis.

- Tiger Woods, a self-described "Caublinasian" (reflecting his diverse ethnic background), defeated New Zealander Grant Waite to win the Canadian Open.

- Sammy Sosa, from the Dominican Republic, hit his major league leading 48th home run. Of course the Cubs lost to Houston because the Astos' Richard Hidalgo, from Venezuela, hit two home runs.

- Randy Johnson, a six-foot-eight-inch left-handed pitcher with hair hanging over his shoulders, struck out 14 batters to become the 12th pitcher in history to reach 3,000 strikeouts.

- Two older (by football standards) white males, Al Del Greco of the Tennessee Titans and Jason Hansen of the Detroit Lions, kicked last-second field goals to win games.

You'll find more talent and get better results when you look for it among people with diverse backgrounds, interests, and appearances. The broader you search, the more talent you're likely to find. Once you recognize this, you can learn to love the differences among people. When people see this from you, they'll feel engaged by it. They'll want to stay and perform for you.

Searching far and wide for talent and accepting differences is happening with much greater frequency on the field in sports. The NHL used to be about 95 percent Canadian and 5 percent American. Now it's 50 percent Canadian, 33 percent European, and 17 percent American. Without European talent, the league could not have expanded throughout North America.

Foreign born and educated players have become the rage in basketball too, a game invented in America. The 2002 rookie of the year, Pau Gasol, is from Spain. The number one draft pick in 2002 was Yao Ming, a seven-foot-six-inch center from China, and two of the other top seven picks were foreign born. Three Europeans play extensive minutes for one of the best teams in the league, the Sacramento Kings.

Even baseball, our national pastime, gets about 25 percent of its players from outside the United States. Baseball's sensation in 2001 was Ichiro Suzuki of the Seattle Mariners, the AL Rookie of the Year and the first Japanese position player to star right away in major league baseball. As my younger son said, "You know you're big when everyone knows you by your first name." Everybody associated with baseball learned who Ichiro is.

Ichiro was a seven-time batting champion in Japan who was extensively scouted and courted by the M's. The team had to pay Ichiro's Japanese team millions just to negotiate a contract with him, even before he signed. But what an investment! In his first year in the major leagues, he helped lead the M's to the division title and the record-tying 116-win season. He won the batting title, hitting .350, and had 242 hits, the most in 71 years. He hit .600 in Seattle's playoff victory against Cleveland and played the best right field in the American League, winning the gold glove. He had another all-star season in 2002.

Talent is everywhere; you just have to take the risks to find it. Kurt Warner, who quarterbacked the Rams to the Super Bowl championship, played at a small college, bounced around the Arena Football League and NFL Europe, and was making his living as a grocery store clerk when he got a tryout with the Rams. After he emerged as a starter and led them to victory, he signed a long-term contract for more than $40 million.

The New York Giants made it to Super Bowl XXXV because they took a risk on Kerry Collins. Collins was a number one choice at the start of his career and had early success with the Carolina Panthers, but in his third year he created a number of problems. He drank heavily and made a racial joke that outraged his black teammates. His coach released him the next year after he thought Collins quit on the team.

Collins tried again for a short while with New Orleans, but he was still drinking. Mike Ditka cut him, and Collins was lost. The NFL ordered him to get treatment for alcoholism and it turned his life around. The next season the Giants signed him to a contract. Wisely, the team brought him along slowly, alternating him with another quarterback while he put his life back together. He emerged during the 2000 season to have one of the most productive seasons of any QB in Giants' history.

Even the last on-the-field taboo, the black quarterback, has been broken, but only in recent years. After decades of converting talented black college quarterbacks, like Tony Dungy and Marlin Briscoe, to defensive backs and wide receivers, teams have learned that black QBs win games. Until the late 1990s, only Doug Williams, James Harris, and a few others were allowed to play the glamour position. Warren Moon refused to play defense, so he had to go to Canada and establish his reputation as a QB there first.

In fact, most of the nine black QBs who started on September 10, 2000 were drafted in 1998 or 1999. Only a few played in the league before then. What caused the change?

The answer's simple. Just like in business, competition in the NFL is more intense. Coaches lose their jobs faster if they don't win. As a result, they've become color blind, choosing the best player instead of letting skin color and ignorance get in the way. Frank Gilliam, the now retired Vikings' vice president of player personnel said it best, "As the emphasis gets more on winning, guys start losing all these biases they had about quarterbacks. Coaches want to win, so they get whoever can win for them."[15] Five of the 12 teams that made the NFL playoffs in 2000 started black QBs.

ON-THE-FIELD, OFF-THE-FIELD

There is a glaring contrast between the on-the-field search for talent that now covers the world and the off-the-field talent hunt for management positions that barely gets beyond white owners' comfort levels. Not only is it racist, it hinders performance. *Limiting the talent pool limits your opportunities for high performance.* Maybe that explains why there's so much turnover among coaches and managers. Maybe it also helps to explain why there's so much turnover among CEOs.

Among the major team sports, the NBA has done the best job of promoting diversity. Of course, it has the highest concentration of black players. At the start of the 2002–2003 season, 13 of the 29 teams had black coaches and several African-Americans worked as executives in the front offices.

Baseball talks a good game about increasing diversity, including starting an equal opportunity committee of owners, but has shown only a little progress. Seven minority managers started the 2002 season—six blacks and one Hispanic. Three more Hispanic managers were hired during the season. This is the most ever, but not nearly enough, given the makeup of the players. And at the end of the season, it appeared that things were slipping back. A few of the minorities were fired and according to Felipe Alou, who had managed the Expos successfully during the 1990s, opportunities were fading. Alou said, "That's the new trend, to have white and young managers. Blacks and Latinos won't have many opportunities from now on."[16]

Ironically, Alou was hired to manage the Giants shortly after making the statement. Still, he was correct. Ten new managers were hired after the 2002 season. Only Alou and Dusty Baker, who changed teams, were people of color.

Among the 30 teams, only the White Sox and the Expos had minority general managers in 2002. These were only the third and fourth in major league history. The Sox and Expos also are the first and only teams with minority general managers and field managers at the same time. At the start of 2002, only one woman was president of a baseball team, Wendy Selig-Prieb of the Brewers, and she got her job the old-fashioned way. Her dad, Bud, gave it to her when he became full-time commissioner. At the end of another disastrous Brewers season in 2002, she kicked herself upstairs to be chairman and gave the presidency to the first minority team president in baseball.

Most embarrassing is pro football. In 2002, approximately 70 percent of the players were black. Yet among the 32 teams, only two blacks were head coaches, Herman Edwards and Tony Dungy. October 9, 2000, when Dennis Green's Vikings played Dungy's Bucs, was the first time in league history when the opposing coaches and quarterbacks both were black. There is one black person running a team's front office, Ozzie Newsome of the Ravens.

At the end of the 2000 season, nine head coaching jobs were open. The men who had been acting as interim coaches filled two of the jobs. There were three black co-coordinators, the step below head coach, who were outstanding candidates for the seven other jobs. But only one, Herman Edwards, was hired. Several Buffalo Bills players endorsed defensive co-coordinator Ted Cottrell for head coach, but he was passed over for a white assistant from another team. Marvin Lewis built the defense that won the Super Bowl, but he didn't get a head coaching job either. In fact, he only got one preliminary interview, also with Buffalo.

After the last vacancy was filled, the press offered its usual out-cries and the league gave its customary, lame excuses. Lewis, like Dungy years before him, was accused of not interviewing well. But the opinions of Green and Dungy were clear—race was the issue. Speaking of Lewis, Dungy said, "You would have thought more than one team out of nine would say that here's a guy that should at least be talked to. And you can only beg the question in your own mind: If he were white, would it have been one out of nine? I don't think so."[17]

I don't think so either. If you're going to engage people, you have to engage everyone. In fact, in September 2002, attorney John-nie Cochran filed a report and threatened a lawsuit against the NFL asserting bias in hiring. Cochran produced statistics showing that black head coaches had been very successful when given the op-portunity. He alleged that black coaching candidates were being held to a "higher standard" for getting jobs.[18]

The NFL said it was trying to do better, but actions always speak louder than words. The NFL's response was just like a re-cent study of large businesses by executive search firm Korn Ferry. Korn Ferry found that while 75 percent of a broad sample of corpo-rate executives believed their own organizations were effective in achieving diversity, less than half of the minority professionals who worked at these companies agreed.[19] The employees wanted to see real results.

The more diverse the talent pool, the more skills become avail-able. Research shows companies with a higher percentage of women and minorities in leadership positions have better business results. More diverse people lead to more diverse thought, and this means greater innovation and more receptivity to a bigger group of cus-tomers. What business wouldn't benefit from that?

LIVES IN THE BALANCE

Sports careers don't last that long, and they often involve a lot of change—from team to team, position to position, player to assistant coach or broadcaster, assistant coach or broadcaster to head coach, and so on. Rarely does anyone stay with one team, play the same position their whole career, and then retire. This is another reason pro sports are a good metaphor for our economy. Employees rarely come to you expecting, or even wanting, to stay their whole careers. You may not want them to either.

The concept of working 30 years for the same company without a break has faded away. Companies killed that, so people now want to reinvent themselves and their careers at various times. At the very least, they want to have periods where they work hard, then take a break to do something else—spend more time with family, travel, etc.—before resuming their previous pace. *Careers aren't linear in time or direction anymore. They're much more likely to be a series of experiences and events.*

To retain skilled people who look at their careers this way, enable them to have a wide variety of experiences while working for you. You can't horde talent to try to keep it in one place doing one thing. You need to let people try out new jobs and career paths, special assignments, new locations, flex time, telecommuting, sabbaticals, compressed work weeks, and other alternatives to traditional careers if that's what they want. This builds their loyalty because they get the variety they want by staying with you.

You may think it's just younger people who see their careers this way, but it's not. Ron Schuler was general manager of the White Sox for ten years. At the end of the 2000 season, at age 52, he decided to step down and return to scouting and consulting for the team. Schuler had just remarried and wanted to cut back on his time commitment and job stress to spend more time with his new wife.

Will Clark saw his career rejuvenate in 2000. In mid-season, the first baseman was traded to the Cardinals to replace the injured Mark McGwire. Clark exceeded all expectations, hitting .345 with 12 home runs and 45 RBIs. But after the season, Clark, 36, surprised everyone by announcing he would retire. Clark said, "I can still hit, I can still play, I can still field my position. The first part of my life was based on being a baseball player. The second part of my life is going to be based on being a daddy and a husband."[20]

Lou Piniella is one of the very best managers in baseball. His ten-year run as manager of the Seattle Mariners brought the team back from mediocrity and financial crisis to become one of the model franchises in the sport. Yet at age 59, after another winning season, he left Seattle with a year on his contract to manage closer to his home in Florida. Piniella explained, "It's just too far to be in Seattle. It's a burden on me, on my family. It's just too far from home."[21]

Golfers Jasper Parnevik, Phil Mickelson, Juli Inkster, and Bruce Lietzke lead by example in this search for balance. Parnevik declined to defend his Bob Hope Classic golf championship in 2001 because his wife was expecting their fourth child. No one could remember a defending champ turning down a tournament for this reason. The Parneviks had a baby boy on the Friday of the Classic. Later that year, Phil Mickelson did much the same thing. He turned down an opportunity to defend his PGA Tour Championship title to stay at home with his brand new daughter. "I'd love to play," he said at the time. "It's a very special tournament and having won last year, it's a tournament I'd love to defend. But right now, the time I'm spending with my family is the most important thing to me, and I wouldn't trade it for anything."[22]

Juli Inkster was Tiger Woods long before Woods. She was the first person to win three straight U.S. amateur titles, ten years before Woods did it. She won two major tournaments in her first year on the LPGA tour and has won seven majors overall. She is the only female golfer of the modern era to win the career grand slam.

Yet according to Ty Votaw, LPGA Tour Commissioner, you can divide Inkster's career into three periods. "There's Juli before kids, Juli just after her kids were born, and Juli now."[23]

Juli was a dominant player before kids. She won 15 titles in the 1980s. Her daughters were born in 1990 and 1994, and from 1990 to 1996 Inkster won only twice. She stopped practicing because she had trouble balancing involved mothering with playing championship golf. Inkster said, "I struggled with it. My mom was a stay-at-home mom."

In 1996, Inkster decided to either play well again or give up golf. She realized that she still could practice a few hours a day and be a good mother. "I finally told myself, 'The kids are loved. They're getting a lot of support.' Once I came to terms with it, I started to put more time into my golf."

Inkster played well again in 1997 and 1998. In 1999 she broke through winning two majors to complete the grand slam and became the LPGA player of the year. She won the women's U.S. Open again in 2002. Inkster's children and their nanny travel with her during the summer, and she plays in fewer tournaments to have more time with family. She takes time off during the winter to be at home and coach her daughters' school teams and turns down appearances that require too much travel. She even carries drawings by her daughters in her golf bag. Now she has struck the right balance and her daughters appreciate that she is one of the best golfers in the world.

Bruce Lietzke carried this even further when he was on the PGA tour. Lietzke began his pro career in 1982 and earned more than $6 million before hitting the senior tour late in 2001. But from 1995 through 2001, he didn't play in more than 16 events per year, usually playing only nine or ten. Instead of playing, he spent his time with his wife and children, taking family trips and coaching the kids' sports teams. He coached and caddied for his teenage son, a good junior golfer, more than he played himself. He played much more in 2002 on the senior tour as his son hit college age.

Lietzke also doesn't spend time practicing. He thinks it just screws up his game. Prior to a tournament, he plays a practice round or two, just to learn the course and get loose. Lietzke prefers to stay mentally fresh by not playing and relies on muscle memory to keep his swing the same as it has been for years. His wife, Rosemarie, loves their lifestyle and having her husband home rather away playing and earning more money. "What would we spend it on?" she asks.[24]

If your employees had Inkster's and Lietzke's resources, they would opt for more balance too. Maybe they can't afford to work part-time or have a nanny so their children can travel with them for work, but they would if they could. They can't, so you need to help them expand their options for their careers and find the balance between work and home life if you want to engage them. Their choices have to make sense for your business, but many leaders go much further now than they thought they could, even a few years ago.

One company that leads the way in helping balancing lives is S.C. Johnson, makers of Johnson Wax, Pledge, Ziploc bags, and other familiar household products. Johnson has shaped its culture around the concept of balance, offering employees a wide range of choices for how they work and support for their families. Johnson's programs include summer hours (Friday afternoons off), an onsite childcare center and other parent support services, a concierge service to help employees handle personal errands, and "no-meeting Fridays" to help employees get more focused work done. These programs pay for themselves because Johnson's annual turnover, including retirements, averages less than 7 percent. Most of the impetus for Johnson's programs comes from the employees themselves—the company runs several highly efficient electronic opinion surveys at any one time to find out what people need and want.[25]

Still, I know a lot of companies with good policies and programs that have leaders who don't believe in them. These leaders believe "face time" is more important than flex time. They don't balance their own lives and send the message to others that they're not hard working or loyal enough if they do. Talented employees resent working for people like this—they hate the loss of control over their work lives.

The more flexible you are about how people do their jobs, the more respect you show for them as individuals. Respect for the individual is what engages and retains people today.

T H E   H U D D L E

If you're a builder:

- Create a development philosophy supported by a set of definable processes and specific plans for each person. Hold yourself accountable for implementing these plans and measure the most important outcomes, like the number of people you prepare for bigger jobs or the number of people who get promoted. Work to increase your numbers.

- Make your calls on whom to develop sooner. Don't wait for people to emerge if they are taking too long. Also recognize that not everyone can be developed to much larger responsibilities. Be realistic about who gets developed for what.

- Cut your losses quickly when you see someone isn't going to make it.

- Regard diversity as a business issue, not as "nice to have" or something that is socially desirable. Measure your progress in diversity, looking at the most important outcomes.

- Insist on business reasons for establishing ways to support work-life balance. "Good for business and good for people" should be the justification for everything you do toward creating more balance.

If you're a driver:

- Understand the need to invest in development to achieve the long-term results you want. Don't immediately cut investments in development when business slows.

- Create a development philosophy supported by a set of definable processes and specific plans for each person. Hold yourself accountable for implementing these plans and measure the most important outcomes, like the number of people you prepare for bigger jobs or the number of people who get promoted. Work to increase your numbers.

- Focus more on the long-term potential of people. Take a little more time to watch it emerge and to help it grow. Don't be afraid to give people a second chance.

- Appreciate that results are blind to color, gender, and demographics. Reach out to a broader group of people who want to pursue your business path regardless of where they started. Bend a little to make them feel valued and celebrate their differences.

- Create a business case and philosophy about work-life balance. Don't just give it "lip service"; apply it and live by it. Make sure others know you think it's important—particularly your star employees.

CHAPTER FIVE

GOALS

Winning Is the Only Thing

"If you're keeping score, win."

—Red Auerbach, former Boston Celtics coach and general manager[1]

ENGAGING WHAT'S REAL

Every company creates a strategy for getting ahead and a business model for enacting that strategy. Obviously, these are essential and if you get your strategy or business approach wrong, you can be in all sorts of trouble. The question for engaging leaders is how much will either of these inspire your employees toward outstanding performance.

You need to remember that for most employees, including some people very high in your organization, your strategy and business model are pretty abstract. These won't matter much to them, unless you can translate them into something real. People are far more concerned with their day-to-day activities. To engage people, you have to address them on a concrete level. Otherwise, you won't get through. They have too many other things on their minds.

Engaging people about what you want to achieve as a business and how you want to do it—getting them excited about getting it done—requires you to create three things: *focus, BHAGs,* and *risk.* These will strike people as real and tangible if you do them right. They can grab people, get them to pay attention, and turn up their energy level for you. They will help your employees understand clearly what you want and what they need to do to help you get there.

FOCUS: AIM HIGH AND KEEP IT SIMPLE

The most engaging leaders and companies have a single-minded focus on what they want to do to win—that's all there is to it. Nothing else matters and they don't let things get in the way. Focus is a direction that people really understand, remember, and follow every day. Sometimes companies call it their mission; sometimes they call it their vision. They might even call it something else. It doesn't matter. What's essential is that the phrase describes in just a few words how you'll achieve greatness through what you're selling or making, who you're selling it to, and what they'll get from it. Employees know they'll win if they stay focused.

Coca-Cola wants to refresh people around the world—everywhere, any time, every day—with its beverages. That sets a platform for worldwide excellence in beverage taste and distribution, along with local marketing built on the notion of enjoyment—quite a lot to convey in just a few words. At Hewitt, we talked about "helping companies and employees succeed together." That meant we tried to provide outstanding service and do things that increased business results and made things better for people. Microsoft says it's about empowering people through great software—any time, any place, and on any device. This is directing Softies to move beyond the PC and develop software for all manners of devices and the Internet.

The words or phrases companies use may be renewed every few years, but the basic purpose and direction of a great company rarely changes, despite new products and improved business models. The best organizations, the ones that have enduring success, don't really change their focus—Microsoft's always been about software even when it only wrote it for PCs. In fact, frequent changes in purpose or direction usually mean you don't have one.

Brian Cashman, general manager of the Yankees, says that after every season the management team sets as its focus winning next year's World Series. Then they evaluate the roster and make the changes they need to do it. That's the team they try to bring into spring training. As the season progresses, they'll make other changes to keep advancing to their goal.[2]

What else could be so powerful and so simple? There's nothing ambiguous about it and nothing to cloud the Yankees' vision. This isn't a new attitude. In 1955, legendary Yankees manager Casey Stengel said, "That's a lot of bunk about them five-year building plans. Look at us. We build and win at the same time."[3]

Compare that to other teams—like the Brewers and Pirates in baseball, Cavaliers and Warriors in basketball, or Cardinals and Bengals in football. Every year these teams tell their fans they're rebuilding to become competitive. Notice they rarely get there?

Now at this point you may be saying, "Sure the Yankees are great, but it's because they spend more money than anyone else." True they spend more, but spending it wisely is what counts. Smart leadership, including a strong farm system and great trades, has been the big factor in the Yankees' success. Though the Yankees have signed a big name free agent almost every year for the last several years, they've spent most of their money to keep the players they've developed.

Meanwhile, the Dodgers and Red Sox, who annually are among the top five payrolls in baseball—some years spending nearly as much as the Yankees—haven't made the playoffs much recently. Conversely, the Giants, Athletics, and White Sox made the 2000 baseball playoffs with below-average payrolls. In 2001, the Astros and Athletics (again) got there without being in the top half of the teams in player salaries. The Athletics (for a third time) and the Twins did it in 2002. The Giants and Angels played in the World Series in 2002 with the 10th and 15th biggest payrolls, respectively. In 2000, the Washington Redskins had the highest payroll in National Football League history and couldn't make the playoffs. The Portland Trail Blazers had the highest payroll in NBA history in 2000–2001, staggered through the season, and were eliminated in the first round.

By itself, spending doesn't guarantee anything. You have to spend smartly. If you don't, it's easy to spend your way into a disaster. If you aim high, you may pay high, but you don't have to be the money leader. The St. Louis Rams, Baltimore Ravens, and New England Patriots won the last three Super Bowls without having the highest payrolls.

Instead, engaging people to win requires you to develop a single-minded, passionate focus on winning. Some might call this a culture of winning. If you're the Yankees, it's referred to as your mystique. Whatever you call it, it's a belief system you instill in your people that winning is what you're about; it's what matters. Help people learn winning is your fundamental value.

To do this, try to distill the key points of your strategy or business model into a few simple, concrete ideas that are easy to communicate to employees. Better yet, do it in a few key words. If you can't do this, things may be too complicated for other crucial audiences—

like customers or shareholders—to understand as well. To help companies with this, I usually ask clients, "What can customers get from you that they can't get anywhere else?" This is your competitive advantage. Unfortunately, it is a surprisingly difficult question for business leaders to answer. But if you can't answer it, how are you going to win in the marketplace? The answer becomes your rallying cry.

To be an engaging leader, talk about winning in these terms all the time. Help people understand what winning in your world means, what it looks like, what it feels like, and how you'll know when you get there. Talk about it in exciting, upbeat terms. Don't discuss losing. If you're in a rough spot, acknowledge where you are currently—that's reality. Keep your attention and your people's attention straight ahead on winning. Use slogans, symbols, or signs, if they mean something. Also let people know what's in for them as they win. Finally, refuse to accept anything less than ultimate victory, although along the way take small wins and build them into bigger ones. If some employees can't understand that, help them understand or get rid of them.

I know this sounds too simple and unsophisticated, like too much sloganeering. But the most successful leaders I know work this way. The others get too bogged down in complexity. You don't have the luxury of sports with its ready measures of wins and losses, but you need to avoid the quicksand of trying to do and measure too much. If you try to drag people into that trap, they won't follow you.

BHAGS: THE VALUE OF BIG GOALS

Once you've defined winning for your team, then cast it in terms of how you'll measure it and what level of success you demand.

This should be your *big, hairy, audacious goal* (BHAG) that will take you to the top. Jim Collins described BHAGs in his book *Built to Last*[4] as the way visionary companies became and remained successful. I think it's a key way that engaging leaders "think group." Setting the big goal gives you something to inspire people with and to execute against.

Winning starts with a BHAG: to be the biggest, to have the highest quality, to be number one in your market, to win the championship, however you define coming out on top. But make sure your BHAG is in sync with your competitive differentiation. Wal-Mart's everyday low pricing makes sense for its BHAG of becoming the biggest merchant in the world. It wouldn't make sense if Wal-Mart tried to offer the best service. For one thing, there aren't enough people to hire to supply that service. For another, Wal-Mart would have to raise prices to pay for more help, and this would price it out of some people's reach. If you want to be large, you have to be low cost.

Make your BHAG simple so people can understand it, very ambitious so they have to stretch hard to reach it, and keep it to one thing. Then align all your resources, tools, and systems so you get it. Research is very clear that if you focus on just one goal, you're more likely to hit it than if you dilute your attention. Don't make it impossible to accomplish or you won't be able to enlist your people. But "close to impossible" is probably where you should aim, as long as you're 100 percent committed. As a friend of mine says, "If you strive for perfection, you'll get excellence."

Setting a BHAG is crucial because it enables you to engage people three ways. First, a BHAG inspires passion in your people. *Quality comes from passion—greatness comes from quality.* Modest goals don't turn on anybody. Andy MacPhail, president of the Cubs, has said on different occasions, "We're committed to being competitive."[5] How passionate is that? Not very passionate because the team is almost never any good. You energize people by getting them to dream about becoming the best and convincing them you're ready to help them get there. Intensely passionate people win. A BHAG will fire up your people.

The second purpose for setting a BHAG is to provide *meaning* to your people and situation. No one wants to work or play for no good reason—it deadens the spirit and the soul. Have you ever sat in the stands late in the baseball season with your team hopelessly out of the running? Usually, it's as quiet as a mausoleum. The few die-hard fans there are more interested in whether their faces show up on the Jumbotron or who wins the electronic M&Ms race rather than how the team is doing. The players aren't thinking about winning. They're just thinking about adding to their individual statistics or playing for a job for next year.

The *pride* that comes from winning, from being the best, provides meaning all by itself. Setting your BHAG on winning will engage people by giving them the pride, meaning, and identity they seek. According to Philadelphia Flyers' head coach Ken Hitchcock, who led the National Hockey League's Dallas Stars to the Stanley Cup, "Any time you step on the ice, your team needs to have an identity, and that identity should be to want to win."[6]

Third, a BHAG enables you to be an *inspirational* leader. It will give you something to talk to your employees about that will feed their aspirations for greatness. It doesn't matter how charismatic you are. The BHAG will help you fuel your employees' drive and help you be more inspiring.

The 1997 and 1999 Ryder Cups, the biennial competition in which the best golfers from the United States play the best golfers from Europe, exhibit this. The 1997 event was held at Valderrama in Spain. The captain of the Europeans was Seve Ballesteros, the dashing, driving hero of Spanish golf.

Seve's play and personality are the personification of charisma. Notoriously wild off the tee, Seve was known for his amazing ability to scramble his way to winning. His extraordinary save shots from trees, roughs, and bunkers, while smiling all the time, captured people's affection and made him tremendously popular all over the world. Ballesteros was intent on becoming the first European ever to both play on and captain a winning Ryder Cup team, and he wanted to do it on his native soil. This was his BHAG.

By all accounts, the Americans had the better team; they were the 2-to-1 betting favorites. But Ballesteros would not let his team lose. He zipped all over the course in his golf cart with his walkie-talkie, coaching his players constantly, picking them up when they needed it, and calming them down when they were too emotional. He also used his star players in more matches, while the American captain, Tom Kite, used his players more equally throughout the tournament. He was the embodiment of the engaging leader.

The newspaper and magazine stories later said that Seve had "willed" his team to victory. That was the view of the American players too. Tom Lehman, one of the few Americans who played well during the 1997 Cup said, "I'm still totally convinced we have the 12 best players. Today [singles matches] proved that. But put their guys together, and they have magic at their fingertips. The sum is greater than their parts."[7] A huge part of the magic was Ballesteros's zealous leadership.

The Americans wanted revenge in 1999 in Boston. This time their captain was Ben Crenshaw, a marked contrast from Ballesteros. Crenshaw was nicknamed Gentle Ben by the press, a quiet Texan who showed his emotions only at particular times. His game also was different than that of Ballesteros—very businesslike, with a deft putting touch. Before the competition, golf commentators worried that Crenshaw was too low-key to bring home the Cup.

Instead, he turned out to be a great example of a builder who became more engaging.

As in 1997, Crenshaw put a great team together, but the first two days were a disaster. The Americans were down 10–6, facing almost certain defeat. Winning required them to take 8½ points of a possible 12 on Sunday to capture the Cup.

On Saturday night, Crenshaw called his team together and gave them a stirring speech about their destiny, his belief in their abilities, and his confidence that it was their fate to win, despite the odds. This was his intervention—his passion in the heat of battle. He later recounted his remarks to the press, "I'm going to leave y'all with one thought. I'm a big believer in fate. I have a good feeling about this."[8]

Then he sent his six best players out first and they swamped the Europeans. The U.S. team won back the Cup, 14½ to 13½. With his BHAG in sight, Gentle Ben was able to inspire his troops to overcome a huge obstacle and beat the Europeans.

Golfers are the ultimate free agents. They earn only as they win, and the more they win, the more they earn. They decide how many and in which tournaments to play, at whatever level they compete. Only rarely do they compete on teams, like in the Ryder and President's Cups. Typically, they are on their own. But these free agents responded powerfully to BHAGs. Imagine what BHAGs can do to engage your employees.

ENEMIES OF BIG GOALS

Big goals are audacious. They take courage to set and pursue. Many times the forces of mediocrity will pressure you to stay away from them. But to engage people, you have to overcome these forces. Caution is the biggest obstacle to BHAGs. It takes courage and self-confidence to fight the fear that predominates in too many business organizations. *Passion breeds courage and self-confidence.* That's why it's an essential characteristic of an engaging leader.

There are two other enemies of BHAGs worth discussing so you can avoid them: mixed messages and lack of vision.

Mixed Messages

Mixed messages occur when you say one thing and do another. People won't believe your goals if you surround them with mixed messages. The 2000 Chicago Bears sent out a ton of mixed messages.

In 1999, the Bears drafted quarterback Cade McNown in the first round and signed him to an expensive contract. McNown played sporadically that year, showing flashes of excellent play, amid plenty of rookie mistakes. McNown also showed a difficult personality for someone who needed to become the team's on-the-field leader. He missed part of training camp while holding out for more money, so he fell behind in learning the offense while the team waited for him. When things went wrong, he tended to blame his teammates rather than take responsibility himself. He often veered from the offensive plan to try to make something spectacular happen, throwing off the precision the Bears were trying to achieve in their passing game. Other players appreciated his competitiveness, but didn't see enough of the collaboration needed among football teammates. He also didn't form many close ties with his offensive mates, often skipping the dinners they had together once a week. The result was this supposed leader didn't earn the trust of his fellow Bears.

When McNown wasn't playing, Jim Miller and Shane Matthews, two experienced, journeymen quarterbacks, ran the team. Matthews did an adequate job and was much more disciplined than McNown. Miller, however, excelled. He gave the Bears the leadership they needed and a big arm to throw the ball downfield. The team really responded during the games in which he played. Unfortunately, just as Miller was asserting himself, he tested positive for steroids from an over-the-counter vitamin supplement he was taking. He claimed he didn't know steroids were in the product but took responsibility and sat out the last four games of the season.

When training camp for the 2000 season came, the Bears' coaches made two things clear. McNown, not Miller, would be the quarterback, and they thought McNown gave them the best chance to win. This was a mixed message because the Bears' players knew better. They thought Miller was their key to victory. As one Bears veteran said, "As crazy as it sounds, we think we can win a Super Bowl with Jim Miller."[9] If the coaches had said McNown was going to play so he could develop and become a star in the long term, that would have been a clear direction. But to position McNown as the starter and say this was the way to win was confusing at best and a lie at worst.

The 2000 season bore this out. McNown was lousy and led the team to a dismal record of one win and seven losses in the first half of the season. Then he went down with an injury. Miller started the ninth game against a tough Indianapolis team and led the Bears to an upset victory. Most of the players were quick to credit Miller for the spark and confidence he gave them. But Jim Miller is just an unlucky guy. He was injured for the season in the following game against Buffalo. The team beat Tampa Bay in its next game on a cold day in Chicago with Matthews at QB. After that game, McNown was healthy and the team vacillated between him and Matthews. The Bears drifted the rest of the season.

Some of the problems may have come from a string of injuries to a team that wasn't deep with talent, despite the fifth highest payroll in the NFL. But another problem may have been the comments Bears Coach Dick Jauron made on his radio show after Miller took over. In response to a question, Jauron insisted there had been open competition for the starting QB job in training camp before the 2000 season. Yet the team and the fans in Chicago had seen a different picture. Jauron's comments were the talk of the city's sports world for a while, including the players on his team, and his credibility was shot.

Mixed messages will blow your credibility. When that happens, your integrity as a leader is gone. All you can do is start over.

In 2001, Jauron had to start over rebuilding credibility with his players. He managed to do it and was helped when the team hired a strong new general manager who got rid of McNown and several other nonperforming players prior to the season. But Jauron created several other problems. He picked Matthews over Miller to start the season because Matthews was less likely to make mistakes, even though the team clearly showed more life with Miller. He also kept some very talented rookies on the bench.

As it turned out, some of the players Jauron wanted to start got injured or didn't perform well in early games. Miller took over at quarterback when Matthews went down and immediately sparked the team to several wins in a row and a few talented rookies were pressed into playing, even though Jauron didn't like how they performed in practice. It seemed as if the right people got to play, regardless of the coach's decision.

Jauron showed why his style is almost "pure" builder. He's extraordinarily patient, often sticking to his plan, like with McNown, regardless of the results. He's very cautious and quiet, slow to tackle problems, and appears to wait for problems to solve themselves.

Still, he's very dedicated to his players and assistants, treats them very consistently, and they like him. This helped him rebuild trust in 2001. Then, finally, he demonstrated some versatility. He flashed some anger at the team during halftime of a game against Minnesota early in 2001, and it woke them up. The Bears went on a winning streak and had their best season in many years.

Lack of Vision

Lack of vision is the other enemy of big goals. *Big goals come from vision.* Lack of vision is related to lack of courage, but it's also different. Vision enables you to see the future so you can form a big goal. Courage helps you state it publicly and stick to it. Without vision, you will be unable to create big goals.

Some leaders look to the future and form vision statements instead of big goals. Personally, I think big goals have more impact on employees than vision statements. I've consulted with several successful companies that didn't have vision statements per se, but instead had BHAGs. The BHAGs were more short term and less lofty than vision statements, but they energized and mobilized people. The BHAGs also were more concrete and simple than the vision statements companies usually write, so engaging leaders could use them to greater effect in directing people. Finally, the BHAGs were easier to stick to because they were less complicated and more action-oriented.

When you lack the vision and courage to form big goals and stick with them, you often end up with band-aid approaches to problems. You think a little fix here and a little fix there will make you well, when radical surgery is needed. If you were intent on pursuing a big goal, you clearly would see the need for major surgery.

You can look at any perennial loser and see this pattern. We can go back to the Cubs for a perfect example. When Andy McPhail came to Chicago to run the team, he set a big goal of rebuilding the team for the long run by creating a great farm system and developing terrific young talent. But McPhail and general manager Ed Lynch continuously traded away good young players for veterans with limited talents whom they thought could help in the short term. They couldn't resist the temptation of a quick fix. Promising youngsters like Doug Glanville and Jon Garland left for little in return. Even after Lynch left, the pattern continued.

This created big holes in the lineup. So every year the team bought a few veteran free agents to plug the holes. Typically, these weren't the best players at their positions, because the best players don't want to play for a loser, and like most losers, the Cubs found reasons not to pursue the best, even though they spent a lot of money. Usually, the club hung on to one or two promising rookies, but because the rookies weren't in an atmosphere of excellence, they didn't learn how to win. The easiest way to learn to win is to imitate successful people who live in a culture of winning. The team told its fans it was on the road to success with each of its moves, but it didn't happen. The Cubs lost 94 or more games four times between 1997 and 2002. Patchwork is never enough. Band-aids don't cure big illnesses.

The Cubs have followed this pattern so long it's their accepted way of operating. Cubs fans no longer expect to win; they just go to Wrigley Field to have a good time at the beautiful, old ballpark. Everyone else knows it too. Pat Gillick, the highly successful general manager of teams in Toronto, Baltimore, and Seattle interviewed for the Cubs general manager's job in 1987. He opted out of the process saying, "I didn't think the Cubs wanted to win. That's part of the marketing plan. Some of the mystique of the Cubs is ineptitude. If they win, there might be an expectation level to win again."[10]

Other long-time losers in business and sports act just like the Cubs. They lack the vision and courage to see that commitment to a BHAG of excellence, supported by major changes in the way they operate, is necessary to break the cycle of losing. On the other hand, you can turn around your team pretty quickly if you set a BHAG and move fast. Especially today, when you can get new talent, communicate new directions, and develop new processes in shorter cycles, it's possible to accelerate change if you commit to breakthrough. Every year a few companies rise to the top after being on death watch just a few years earlier.

Take a cue from Jack Nicklaus if you want to be an engaging leader—believe it, and then do it. Success will follow. Nicklaus once listed his ten tips for outstanding putting. Then he added an 11th: No matter how impossible the putt, if you believe you're going to make it, you probably will.[11] That's setting a BHAG, casting aside your doubts, and doing what it takes to win.

RISK: DO IT BIG, DO IT ALL, DO IT FAST

When Mickey Mantle died, *Sports Illustrated* wrote a great tribute to him. One of the memorable lines in the story was, "The world will always belong to those who swing from the heels."[12]

Hitting your big goal of winning almost always requires taking major risk, swinging from the heels like Mickey did. How big the risk depends on how far you are from your goal. Usually you're further than you think.

The New Jersey Devils were, arguably, the best team in the National Hockey League late into the 1999–2000 season. The Devils led the Eastern Conference and were first in the league in points (a team gets two points for a win and one for a tie) when the team went into a brief slump. Players started showing some bad habits under coach Robbie Ftorek, playing more like individuals than a team. General manager Lou Lamoriello sensed trouble and an early exit from the playoffs if things continued this way. He saw that the team was further from the Stanley Cup than anyone else thought.

What did Lou do? He swung from his heels and fired Ftorek with eight games left to go in the regular season. Lamoriello replaced him with assistant Larry Robinson, who didn't want to be head coach. Robinson had been there and done that in Los Angeles, and was fired for his efforts. He had been known as a very tough player, but some saw him as a soft, "player's" coach. Yet the hard-driving Lamoriello has a reputation as a terrific judge of talent. He believed Robinson could be an engaging leader who could bring the discipline and "team first" ethic the Devils needed.

For his part, Robinson redefined the team, got them playing together, and led them to a Stanley Cup victory over Dallas in a classic, defense-oriented series. Why did he make such a risky move? Lamoriello explained, "Good is not good enough, when better is expected."[13]

The impatient Lamoriello struck again in 2001 when the Devils struggled. He replaced Robinson, with a hardcore driver, Kevin Constantine, who coaches much like Ftorek does. Constantine got the team playing better, and later in the season the Devils even brought back Robinson as an assistant coach. When the Devils didn't get to the Stanley Cup final, Lou fired Constantine and brought in Pat Burns, a three-time NHL coach of the year.

Actually, this pattern of alternating drivers and builders repeats itself frequently in sports and business. People hiring leaders often replace a person with someone who has complementary strengths and style. They just keep switching to try new leaders until one fits. Instead, they should look at how versatile and engaging the new leader is, rather than the style of leadership.

When Dick Vermeil coached the St. Louis Rams, he took a huge risk to win Super Bowl XXXIV. Getting the ball back with the game tied 16–16 and 2:05 remaining in the fourth quarter, Vermeil knew all his team had to do was to move down the field slowly, kill the clock, and kick a field goal to win. His entire coaching experience told him this was the right thing to do. Still, all season long, the Rams won by throwing the ball deep, trusting offensive coordinator Mike Martz's wide-open attack. On first down, Martz called a long sideline pass. Vermeil, a notorious driver, sure of his ways, hesitated. But then, as hard as it is for a driver to delegate and give up control, he went with Martz's play. Quarterback Kurt Warner hit wide receiver Isaac Bruce for a 73-yard touchdown and a 23–16 lead.

The size of Vermeil's risk became evident as the Tennessee Titans got the ball and drove down the field against the Rams. Tennessee quarterback Steve McNair led the Titans almost all the way to a touchdown. Only a last second tackle by the Rams' Michael Jones at the 1-yard line stopped the Titans short of scoring and winning. Later, Vermeil replayed his agony over trying for the big play with that much time left. He concluded that because he had relied on Martz all season, he couldn't justify abandoning him at the big moment.[14]

RISK REQUIRES ANTICIPATION, INNOVATION, AND SACRIFICE

Like Lamoriello and Vermeil, successful leaders, whether drivers or builders, take risks. Sometimes risk is just about business.

Sometimes it's personal, and when it is, it usually involves stepping beyond your style. The payoff is you become more versatile and engaging by doing so. Drivers do it when they give up control; builders do it when they grab more of it.

Many of your best employees are risk takers. That's one of the reasons they're your best. They respond well when you get out of your comfort zone and show the determination and courage necessary to win by taking the right risks.

Successful risk taking demands several things. First, it requires *anticipation.* You have to be able to look ahead and see where things are likely to go, and then move quickly to get there first. Lamoriello anticipated problems for the Devils in the playoffs when teamwork and defense become keys to victory. Devils' defenseman Ken Daneyko said Robinson's hiring was a necessary move. "We were probably headed for another early exit. But when they brought Larry in, guys started pulling together instead of pulling apart."[15] Much of that was attributed to Robinson's calm, disciplined style that earned the respect of the players.

Risk means *innovation,* like Vermeil and Martz's offense. You have to try new things. No team had ever spread the field more or attacked opponents with greater speed than the Rams. Other teams just couldn't catch up to them in 1999. They were the first team to defy convention and win the Super Bowl by relying on offense, not defense.

Vermeil also took a big risk with Warner, who, until then, had been an Arena Football League quarterback. No one had ever made the jump from arena football to starting in the NFL. When Trent Green, an expensive free agent, was injured in training camp, Vermeil didn't panic and trade for a veteran replacement. He figured if Warner could star in the accelerated pace of the AFL, then he should be able to make speedy decisions and release the ball quickly as the spread offense demanded. In fact, Vermeil said Warner wasn't a great practice player but was terrific under game pressure. Warner turned out to be the perfect fit for the Rams' fast-strike offense.[16]

Risk also means *sacrifice* because you often have to give up something you're already doing well. You have to trust that you can reeducate yourself and others. When Phil Jackson coached the Bulls, he realized teams could focus so much on stopping Michael Jordan that the Bulls would be good enough to make the playoffs but couldn't win championships. It took a while, but Jackson persisted and persuaded Jordan to sacrifice parts of his individual game, trust his teammates, and get them involved. It often was a struggle for Jordan to let less talented players assume leading roles, but he was able to do it enough to win six championships. In two of those championships, John Paxson and Steve Kerr hit the winning shots in the final games.[17]

The three cornerstones of risk—anticipation, innovation, and sacrifice—require trust in yourself and your skills and trust in others to get the job done. Not coincidentally, *your employees define success as being trusted to do their jobs well.* When you trust people, you create possibilities for them to do great things. Your trust liberates them, and they'll respond by achieving your BHAGs.

RISK ENERGIZES EMPLOYEES

Trust is one reason risk energizes employees. Other reasons are the excitement risk brings and the role model you set for your employees. Most people love the action created by a good bet. Taking a smart risk at work is like that. Plus, when people see you doing it, they know they can take a chance too in the right situation. Taking a risk to meet your BHAG is an extraordinarily powerful way to energize your team. But energy sustains only if you're willing to keep taking risks when they're needed. We can see this in examples from Jerry Manuel and Dennis Green who didn't keep it going.

Jerry Manuel took a risk when he jump-started the Chicago White Sox to the 2000 American League Central Division championship. It gained him the AL manager of the year honors. Manuel did it in spring training by challenging his biggest star, slugger Frank Thomas, to become a better team player. The year before, Thomas had a down year at the plate and was preoccupied by personal problems and injuries. He seemed aloof from his teammates and sulked at some of the criticism he received.

Early in training camp, Manuel was running the team through sprint drills. Thomas didn't want to do them, claiming a sore toe. Manuel is a soft-spoken, philosophical builder, given to the long view. The season before, he didn't confront Thomas and the situation got away from him. Obviously, Manuel came to spring training with a different mind-set, focused and ready to go to war with his star if that's what it took. When Thomas complained about doing the drills, Manuel got in Thomas's face in front of everyone—players, coaches, and the press. He insisted Thomas participate like his teammates. They started arguing and took their fight into a private room to reach an accommodation. After Thomas proved the toe really hadn't healed from an earlier injury, Manuel announced Thomas would do the drills as soon as he was ready, and he did.

By making sure Thomas knew the team came first but enabling him to back down gracefully, Manuel thought group but saw the individual. It was the defining moment in bringing the team together and getting it off to a fast start. It was a moment of versatility for Manuel.

According to Manuel, "Commitment means changes, and sometimes change is uncomfortable. If you're going to be committed to winning a world championship, you have to be willing to change. Because the White Sox haven't won one . . . I'm here to change them."[18] What he didn't say was he also had to change himself. Change starts at the top—you have to be adaptable to be engaging.

Coach Dennis Green took a different kind of risk to reenergize his Vikings before the 2000 football season. Green's team went 15–1 in 1998 but blew the National Football Conference championship game against the Atlanta Falcons. In 1999, the Vikings slipped to 10–6, barely making the playoffs. They lost badly in the semi-finals to the eventual champion Rams. Green knew the team was headed in the wrong direction.[19]

Green's a builder who was intensely loyal to many players. He gave them a very wide berth about performance and behavior, both on and off the field, and shielded them from the criticism that accompanies this. People, particularly in the press, expect professional athletes to act a certain way. Green believes in letting people be themselves.

Yet, before the season Green felt the team's chemistry was all wrong. Coaches weren't together in their thinking and didn't communicate well. Some veteran players were more concerned about themselves rather than the team. Green said, "We had a lot of guys focused on individual agendas."[20]

In response, Green drew a hard line and made huge changes. He got rid of his offensive and defensive co-coordinators and several other assistants, let go of two Pro Bowl offensive linemen and cut several other veterans and replaced them with people he thought more closely shared his point of view. Green increased the focus on his way to play and everyone's accountability for performance by taking such drastic action.

But the biggest risk Green took was getting rid of his veteran quarterbacks, Randall Cunningham and Jeff George, and handing the team over to untested Daunte Culpepper. In 1998, Cunningham led the Vikings to its 15–1 season and was the league's player of the year. George took over for Cunningham midway through the 1999 season, was 8–2 as a starter, and added a playoff victory before the loss to the Rams. In fact, Culpepper only played one down as a rookie in 1999.

Still, Green felt Culpepper had all the physical and mental tools to be successful. Plus, his huge size gave Green an additional power runner, an unknown characteristic at QB. Above all, Green believed in the talent he assembled around Culpepper and his offensive system. He had a right to be confident. His teams had gone to the playoffs seven times in eight years with six different QBs.

The Culpepper risk was a huge success. He became a star almost from his first game. He led the team to an 11–5 record, a playoff win and the National Football Conference championship game, and was voted the starting quarterback for the Pro Bowl. Culpepper had been a controversial draft choice because the Vikings badly needed defensive help, but his size, mobility, and strong arm ushered a new type of quarterback into pro football.

However, the inability to sustain this kind of risk taking and versatility cost both Green and Manuel. I've already described how the Giants pummeled the Vikings in the NFC title game, a game that sent the team into a freefall. The trouble signs had been there all throughout the second half of the season as the team struggled after a very strong start. But Green never stepped up to take dramatic action to refocus the team and put a little fear into his players who needed it. Chris Carter, then the team leader, said, "We play our best when we're a little scared. When we get overconfident, we don't play well."[21] By the next season, the whole team was in disarray, and Green resigned just before being fired.

Manuel reverted to his usual building style in spring training in 2001. This time Thomas threw a fit over his salary and walked out of camp, but Manuel didn't take him to task. First he covered for Thomas and then let the situation play out on its own. Newly arrived pitcher David Wells came in with a back injury and Manuel allowed the veteran to go his own way with workouts. When Thomas got off to a slow start because of injuries early in the season, Wells started questioning his toughness and leadership in the press, even though Wells wasn't pitching very well. Again, Manuel seemed to let it go.

By this time the Sox ship was sinking. The team was losing. Then Thomas, Wells, and several other pitchers were lost for the season to injuries. When Wells went down, Thomas said it was karma. Soon, a team that was expected to win its division was hopelessly out of the race, 15 games under .500 by late May.

But in mid-June the team righted itself and went on to a winning season. Some of it was just getting reorganized after all the injuries. But the typically patient Manuel also had to shake things up to get it going. The Sox started to win after Manuel openly discussed breaking up the team through trades, benched two star players for lack of effort, and criticized them publicly. "I was criticizing, they were criticizing, I was jumping on guys," Manuel said. "That's a part of a team maturing. There are certain things that have to be confronted. A lot of times you don't want to confront someone when they're down, but you want to know that you can confront him when you're not getting the effort."[22]

What would have happened if Manuel had confronted Thomas, Wells, and the rest of the team in spring training when things started to go bad? Could he have avoided the slow start despite the injuries? Who can say for sure? But chaos surrounded the team from the start and wasn't replaced by order until June.

RISK TAKERS NEED SUPPORT

A word of warning: Before you take these kinds of risks make sure you have someone covering your back. Nobody succeeds alone. Even the most successful leaders need support. Whenever you see someone taking risks and winning, you see a strong person helping. This may be someone who reports to you, a boss who believes in you, or an independent-minded board member. When I coach leaders to be more engaging, we always identify a supporting person who can help monitor the changes, give feedback and provide some cover if problems arise.

Whoever it is, *your support person needs to help you think things through clearly, tell you what you need to hear—not what you want to hear—and give you emotional aid when times get tough.* Find someone who can give you this kind of help. Few of us are smart enough or tough enough to change all by ourselves. The people who think they need the least help are the ones who often need the most.

It's much more effective when your support person has the style opposite from yours. He or she will see the world from a different perspective and complement your viewpoint. This can help you become broader and more versatile.

Joe Torre, a builder, gets his help from Don Zimmer, a driver. Zimmer is a baseball lifer, with more than 50 years as a player, coach, and manager. Zimmer has sat next to Torre on the Yankee bench during all of the championship seasons, dispensing advice and opinions that keep Torre steps ahead of opposing teams.

Bobby Cox, another builder, has led the Atlanta Braves to eleven straight division titles, a record that's unmatched, built on a foundation of fabulous pitching. His number two man has been Leo Mazzone, his pitching coach and a driver. Watching the two is a study in contrasts. Cox is calm and low key. Mazzone paces, chews gum constantly, and maintains a steady conversation with Cox, his pitchers on the bench, and the guys in the bullpen. He is the fire to Cox's ice in the Braves' dugout.

Phil Jackson has depended on long-time assistant coach Tex Winter. Winter, now in his late 70s, invented the triangle offense Jackson loves. More than that, Winter provides players with a counterbalance to Jackson's approach to coaching. Jackson is highly psychological, symbolic, and subtle, often accused of being a "master manipulator." Winter is straightforward and direct. Jackson gets in people's faces when he has to—Winter does it all the time. Winter was one of the few people who didn't get caught in the middle of the Bulls' feud between Jackson and general manager Jerry Krause. Winter told each of them exactly what he was thinking without holding back. He played no favorites and wanted no favors. When Jackson left the Bulls, he hired Winter to come with him to the Lakers.

Leading and taking risks without any support, or surrounding yourself only with people who won't challenge you, will prove deadly. You have to have someone with a different view to help you think about all the possibilities, including an exit strategy if things don't work out. Ed Lynch discovered this as general manager of the Cubs.

The 2000 season was another miserable year for the Cubs. In July, Lynch started talks with the Yankees about trading slugger Sammy Sosa. Sosa is not only the star of the Cubs, but also extremely popular in New York, which has a large population from Sammy's home, the Dominican Republic. New York City once even threw a ticker tape parade for him.

Sosa, who is very sensitive, found out about the trade talks, went into a funk, and fell into a deep slump at the plate. The Cubs started losing even more than usual. Eventually, the Yankees decided the Cubs wanted too much for Sosa and wouldn't trade.

Now Lynch was in real trouble. When the trade talks became public, a lot of Cubs fans were outraged that the team would even think about trading its most productive and popular player. After the deal collapsed, Lynch looked foolish and ineffectual. He couldn't make things happen he thought were necessary. Sosa, of course, was delighted. He loves being the hero of Chicago and despised the idea of a trade. After trade talks stopped, Sosa went on a hitting rampage and the team went on a rare winning streak. This made Lynch look even worse.

At this point it became clear Lynch no longer had the support of the fans or his boss, Andy MacPhail. MacPhail had been general manager of the Twins, but once he joined the Cubs as president, he was eager to disengage and kick himself upstairs. If he had given Lynch the go-ahead to explore trading Sosa, he retreated once things went badly. Lynch was left to fend for himself.

After the Sosa fiasco, Lynch and MacPhail agreed Lynch should step down as general manager, move out of town, and become a consultant to the team. As Lynch had operated alone, there was no clear successor. MacPhail took over as general manager and announced his first order of business would be to not trade Sosa. He signed Sosa to an expensive, long-term deal before the start of the 2001 season.

Maybe Lynch could have made a good trade for Sosa, but he didn't have the support from above to help him consider his options clearly. He surely had no support once his plans failed. He had no exit strategy, so he had to exit himself.

MAKING RISK PAY OFF

Legendary baseball executive Branch Rickey was fond of the adage "luck is the residue of design."[23] Of course, you often just need to be lucky. But sometimes taking risks to meet your goals can improve your luck.

The New York Giants were a mediocre football team in 1999 and again in 2001, finishing 7–9 both years. But they had a big year between these seasons during 2000. They got off to a fast start at 7–2 leading their division and surprising everyone by overachieving. Then bad things started to happen. The Giants played poorly and lost two straight games at home, falling behind in the standings to the even more surprising Philadelphia Eagles.

That's when Jim Fassel, their usually steady and measured builder head coach, took his big leap and turned mediocrity into success. During a news conference, Fassel guaranteed, to everyone's surprise, that his team would make the playoffs. With a big smile, he announced, "I'm raising the expectations. I'm raising the stakes. I love it."[24] Then he went upstairs to tell his bosses what he did.

Fassel's boss, Ernie Accorsi, was supportive. "If he feels good about the team's chances, that's great. He has the pulse of his team." Moreover, Accorsi said Fassel's job was not in jeopardy because of what he said. "I don't think that any of the evaluation process will have to do with the words."[25]

Fassel's risky ploy worked for himself and his team. The Giants won seven straight games and captured the National Football Conference championship to make it to the Super Bowl. The team played well above its skill level. His players said Fassel's guarantee pushed them to make it happen. Tackle Lomas Brown said when Fassel offered his guarantee, "I remember we all looked at each other. But it was good. . . . He gave us all tunnel vision and focused us in on winning. It was a stroke of genius on his part."[26]

Part luck, part motivation, Fassel's words were just what the Giants needed to reenergize. Fassel's words also are a good example of how BHAGs require risk taking, and how people respond to them. Giants running back Tiki Barber was clear about that. "We were playing without a lot of enthusiasm. Coach Fassel just put it out there. He's our coach, and we believe in him. He made a goal for us, and we chased it."[27]

Maybe Fassel should have made another guarantee in 2001.

THE HUDDLE

If you're a builder:

- Identify your big way to create success, and insist everyone gets on board with you. Builders often have trouble focusing on just one thing because they don't want to rule out other people's goals and interests. Get over it.

- Take the leap, set a BHAG, and commit 100 percent to it. Create an absolute measure of success. This will feel risky to you. Learn how to live with it.

- Be quicker to grab control of a situation. Don't wait for problems to solve themselves. If you need to confront people, do it sooner. Don't carry the stress yourself—give it back to the people causing it.

- Find a driver in whom you can confide. Use this person as a sounding board to help solve problems. This will give you another perspective on things.

If you're a driver:

- Be sure you're not the only one who feels passion about your direction. It must be meaningful and inspirational to others.

Drivers often are able to focus on one key to business success but they often don't consider how motivating this will be to others. Get everyone involved.

- Be careful not to set your BHAG so high that it's impossible to attain. "Stretch" is good, but don't overdo it. People won't even try if there's no chance of success.

- Be quicker to delegate and empower people. Many drivers are afraid of giving up control. Hire highly skilled people and learn to trust them. If they're good and you don't trust them, the fault may be with you.

- Find a builder in whom you can confide. Use this person as a sounding board to help solve problems. This will give you another perspective on things.

CHAPTER SIX

CHEMISTRY

Trust First

"It's very tough to commit unless you trust."

—New York Yankees manager Joe Torre[1]

CHEMISTRY = TRUST + STRUCTURE

Earl Weaver, the highly successful manager of the Baltimore Orioles in the 1970s and 1980s, used to say, "Chemistry is a three-run homer." On any given day, he was right. Three runs can cure a lot of ills if you're losing a baseball game.

But over the course of a season, a critical project, a fiscal quarter, or longer, things are more complicated. In sports and business, you can assemble all the right talent with all the mental toughness you need, but *unless you build superior chemistry among team members, you won't get far.* You certainly won't hit your BHAG. Good chemistry sparks high performance.

In business, we're used to talking about culture—the shared values that build up over a long time and help guide operating relationships and decision making. Culture is the glue that holds companies together and creates a competitive advantage when you know how to use it. But how do you build a sustaining culture when business conditions change so quickly and people switch jobs as often as they do? Where do you start? How do you create a winning atmosphere quickly, particularly as things and people keep moving?

In sports, coaches are more likely to talk about chemistry, something you can mix faster than culture. Chemistry can start with just two people. A positive chemistry—a chemistry of trust—can be expanded into a climate of trust, one that influences many people. Chemistry and climate lead to a desired culture, if you extend them over time. Engaging leaders start with chemistry to build winning environments.

The two keys to building good chemistry are trust and a structure of clear roles, accountabilities, and rewards. The two are completely interrelated. People have to trust to follow the structure you establish to attain goals. The more trust they feel, the more they'll buy in to how you want to do things. Meanwhile, as your structure creates dependability and success, they'll feel greater trust with you and each other. Increasing trust and creating a more effective structure means more and bigger wins for you. Usually, drivers are better at structure and builders are better at trust. Engaging leaders excel at both.

In this chapter, we'll talk about building trust. Trust requires you to step up, expand your versatility, and use all your person-to-person and small group skills. I'll also tell you how to go beyond trust to engage people further, once trust is in place. In the next chapter, we'll complete the picture by discussing structure.

A SHORT COURSE IN TRUST

People use the word *trust* every day, but it's a challenging concept. It's both how people relate to each other and the outcomes of these relationships. These outcomes are the social climate you create and the concrete results coming from that climate. A trusting climate breeds positive results. Rarely can you get the results you want without trust, and if you do, the results will take much longer to reach and won't last as long.

It takes a while to build trust, but trust can be lost in seconds. Many leaders think they have it in their organizations, but employees don't experience it. It's impossible to quantify in any real way, but easy to identify when it's not there. As leader you must be able to see signs of it, so you can fix it or grow it; but, basically, you'll know trust exists when you and your people feel it.

Employee research says people feel trust when leaders do what they say they are going to do. Most leaders think they do this, but studies say only about half the people in a company trust their leaders. The further down the ladder you go in an organization, the less trust there is. Usually, only about a quarter of the people at the bottom trust the top.[2]

Think about trust as meeting expectations. Mistrust comes from missing expectations. Mistrust occurs when leaders promise too much to people and deliver too little. They create expectations they can't meet. Another problem is a lack of communication; leaders don't say enough about what they're going to do so people fill in the gaps with their imaginations. Few leaders can live up to these kinds of expectations. Leaders who don't get to know their people well and don't let people get to know them suffer from both kinds of problems. The closer you are to your people, the easier you make it for them to build realistic expectations.

Keeping promises is the start of trust, but just doing that doesn't necessarily engage people. We can trust baseball owners to stumble over their own greed in dealing with the players' union, but this doesn't mean we're engaged by their cause. What if people know you'll cut their jobs at the first sign of trouble? You can fulfill their expectations but they may not appreciate it.

To engage people, build trust on a foundation of positive social values. Start with integrity, honesty, and fairness. Employees see these as the cornerstones of trust. Then add caring to the mix. Don't violate any of these four things—ever. This will enable people to look up to you. Remember, people want to work for leaders they admire.

Data on engaging employees show that engaging the spirit is incredibly important to people, and the more education people have, the more important it is. In addition to challenging work and the freedom to do it without much interference, skilled people want to find meaning on the job. My analysis of the data from the best employer surveys shows you can create a spirit of "a day here is a day well spent" by doing two things. First, help your team understand it's producing a valuable product or service for others. As a leader, you can talk about your mission as selling more computers or you can talk about it as making technology easier and more available for people. You can discuss being more efficient in patient care or you can talk about providing more access to health care for more people. In each instance, wouldn't the second approach give your group a stronger sense of purpose?

The best companies and most engaging leaders state their missions clearly, concisely, constantly, and in the context of how it helps others. Their employees "get it" and respond accordingly. That's why Southwest Airlines doesn't talk about itself as a discount airline; it talks about offering great service at low fares so people have the freedom to fly. CDW Computer Centers helps its employees understand they're there to find solutions for their customers' computing problems, whether it's hardware, software, service, or training. Selling more is a way to get there, but CDW won't grow unless these are genuine solutions to real problems.

If employees are going to give you 8, 10, or 12 hours a day, they want to feel their time is worthwhile. People know you're in business to make money. While you have to educate them about how that happens, there's no need to remind them about it every day. Instead, great leaders engage people around a higher purpose to increase motivation and business results. Of course, if you do this you have to mean it and act like it. Don't talk about providing products that improve people's lives and then scrimp on quality or service that customers need.

The second thing to do is help people feel like your team or organization is good for your community. Some of the initiative for this may come from your company, but you don't have to wait. I've seen engaging supervisors create opportunities for volunteering or good deeds at the work team level. These can be good team-building efforts too, like a canned food drive, working in a soup kitchen, participating in a charity walk, and so on. The time spent in these worthwhile activities energizes employees for their work activities and brings a great return on your investment.

These two things enable people to feel like they're contributing to something bigger than themselves. This picks up their spirits and makes them feel special. It helps them trust that you'll act ethically because you have good social values.

Teams take on the personalities of their leaders, so to build trust, be trusting. Start by extending trust to your people. Do this by showing people you expect them to do their jobs well, and then give them plenty of freedom to perform. *Micromanaging is the great enemy of trust.* It signals your doubts about their abilities to succeed. If you had doubts, you shouldn't have hired them or given them the assignment in the first place. Another key to engaging people is giving them opportunities to offer input about how their work should be done. Micromanaging cuts off that involvement and influence.

It makes people feel like they should keep their mouths shut and just take orders. Who wants to feel like that? People need to feel they're working with you, not for you.

Extending trust may take a leap of faith for you, and it requires putting your own ego aside. But you have to go first and show trust if you want to create the right climate. The right environment is one in which people feel they'll be treated fairly and like professionals. A professional is someone who does whatever it takes to get the job done well. A professional leader trusts people to do their jobs successfully. Doing the job well requires engagement or commitment, and that's why Joe Torre linked the two—trust and commitment. When you trust, people will commit to your goals.

Jim Fassel mixed the right chemistry on the way to taking his Giants to Super Bowl XXXV. One of his assistant coaches said, "He picked the right people around him and the right players. He took everyone on a golf outing, on boat trips. He brought the team together and it helped when he stopped being his own offensive coordinator. You can't be a bank president and a teller at the same time."[3] In other words, he focused on creating a friendly social climate and stopped micromanaging.

Create a chemistry and climate of trust by:

- Picking people who have the experience, skills, motivations, and values you want while watching out for big egos.

- Starting with the assumption that people will do their jobs well, or enabling them to do well through education, coaching, and support.

- Allowing people to do their jobs without overmanaging.

- Putting some fun into the mix.

- Sticking with people, even when they make mistakes or get into a slump.

- Recognizing that errors and slumps are for learning, not punishing.

- Taking corrective action if performance is lacking for too long.

J.T. Snow played first base for the 2002 National League Champion San Francisco Giants, and like all his teammates, said manager Dusty Baker was a big reason for the team's success, "He just lets you play . . . you show up and play hard. There are not a lot of rules. We try to have fun and play the game the right way."[4] Earlier, I said employees define success as feeling trusted to do their jobs well. That's what Snow said too.

Baker's building style leads him to get close to his players and become a confidant. He was the sounding board for many Giants and frequently joined them for dinner or socialized with them on the road. His pitching coach, Dave Righetti said, "A lot of managers are afraid to get to know their players. . . . But he gets to know them and tests their personalities a lot . . . though he doesn't let it affect his decision making."[5]

According to Baker, "You have to be able to analyze personalities and mood swings to feel comfortable and confident enough to ask, 'Hey, what's wrong?' Even if a guy says nothing, he might come back and talk to you about it later because he knows you're not going to go around telling."[6]

Still, if you don't take corrective action when needed, you run the risk of losing the people who are performing. They'll feel you're jeopardizing their futures by staying with someone who isn't up to the job. During 2002, when the New York Giants kept playing poorly, Jim Fassel took another risk and started calling plays again. This risk sparked the team like his guarantee in 2000. Players never comment publicly when someone who deserves it gets cut from the team. That wouldn't be right. But people know who wants to win and has the ability and motivation to help the team. That's the person they want on the field with them.

Ultimately, trust comes from dealing with people honestly, particularly when it comes to making changes, critiquing their performance, or setting expectations. Look them in the eye and tell them the truth.

TRUST AMONG PEERS

Trust starts when you extend it and communicate openly with your team. But you also have to make sure trust builds from employee to employee. You do that by establishing strong social ties with your employees and initiating connections among them.

Herm Edwards, coach of the New York Jets, said this is one of the great lessons he learned while playing for Dick Vermeil from 1977 to 1982. Edwards described Vermeil this way, "A lot of coaches are afraid to get close to players. But Dick proved you can foster a relationship with players and still make them accountable. That's going to be his legacy. It won't be so much the Super Bowl he won or the championship games he's been involved in."[7] Vermeil says he always treats his teams like family. That's why "likeability" is important to him. If he doesn't like a player, he can't bring him into the family, and probably the other players won't like him either.

Make sure this communication and closeness occurs between you and your employees and also among your employees. When it goes away, you're in trouble. Sean Lowe said one of the reasons his White Sox team won in 2000 was the bond formed among teammates. This bond helped them get through their toughest times.

Lowe noted, "We've had our horses go down, but this is a team thing. And there's nobody tighter than this team. Everybody is friends. When you're friends the way we are, you just fight harder for one another. You bow your back."[8]

But the bond wasn't there in 2001 as the team slumped. Jerry Manuel said the team had the wrong ingredients in its mix of players. Sox player Paul Konerko described it this way, "It wasn't a bad clubhouse where we were at each others' throats, but we definitely didn't have the chemistry of last year where we had everyone pulling for each other and rallied around each other. I think the injuries were a big part of it, but there were many nights where we had the horses to win the game and maybe that lack of chemistry is the reason why we came out on the short end."[9] In our win-now world, chemistry collapses quickly if success doesn't follow. Sometimes it lasts only a few weeks.

Dennis Green thought he improved the chemistry on the Vikings after the 1999 season. He made several changes to get people to work together better, firing most of his coaches including his offensive and defensive coordinators, and hiring seven new ones. Midway through the 2000 season, everything seemed great.

When the Vikings were 7–0, the staff was singing in harmony and the good feelings flowed to the players in the locker-room. "Everybody communicates well together," said new offensive coordinator Sherman Lewis. "We make sure that everybody's ideas are listened to and utilized because we've got a lot of experience."[10] Charlie Baggett, the receivers' coach, added, "I don't think that there's a guy on this staff that you can say has a problem with another guy. I haven't been on a staff like that before."[11]

However, as the team struggled through the second half of the season, the chemistry evaporated. Though it won its division and made it to the NFC championship, the team went 4–5 after its

7–0 start and then lost big to the Giants, 41–0, in the title game. Everyone was embarrassed by the lack of effort against the Giants and the internal sniping started again. Green's alchemy skills had evaporated.

Phil Jackson experienced the ephemeral nature of chemistry in his first two years with the Lakers. When he arrived in 1999, he spent a lot of time with Shaquille O'Neal understanding him and building the close relationship O'Neal wanted. What Jackson worked on most was getting Shaq to accept Kobe Bryant, whom Shaq seemed to really dislike. All season long, Jackson communicated with O'Neal about the need to work cooperatively with Kobe and the contribution Kobe could make to the team and Shaq's game. Shaq responded and formed an uneasy truce with Bryant. The relationship was smoothed over and things worked during the 1999–2000 season. The Lakers won the NBA title, and the team's media guide cover picture for the 2000–2001 season even showed Kobe and Shaq hugging after they won the championship.

But year two in Los Angeles was much harder, largely due to renewed fighting between O'Neal and Bryant. By the end of January 2001, the team had lost more games than it did during the entire 1999–2000 season. Bryant felt like he turned his game up a notch in 2000–2001 and wanted the offense to run through him. "Everybody expected me to come back and do the same things I did last year. But I've improved so much. I have to prove to myself and the league that I'm a better player."[12] For Bryant, this meant taking more shots and passing the ball less to O'Neal.

Shaq, however, still thought it was his team, "We're not an outside team. We're an inside-out team. You have to get me into the game . . . it doesn't get done if I don't get it."[13] So the two spent most of the first part of the season sniping at each other, rather than their opponents.

Jackson's response was to take a tougher tone with his stars and his team, "the sand box," as he called it. "This is really why I'm here, to fix the tussles with the wills of these guys . . . you've got guys willing to do their thing against the will or maybe the good of the team. What it's all about is how to corral that and make it into a community effort."[14] Veteran player Horace Grant had a simpler description of Jackson's new tone, "ornery and disappointed."[15] Jackson's Zen approach turned into tougher communication to both players, especially Bryant, to try to restore trust. In my terms, he had to become more versatile and act like a driver for a while. The result was the players re-engaged and won another championship.

BIG EGOS DESTROY TRUST

John Wooden, the legendary basketball coach at UCLA, used to say, "The price of glory is the rest of the team." *Individual egos can poison positive chemistry and trust.* This was the road Bryant traveled as he tried to show he was the best player in the league. In the process, he was destroying the trust that had carried the Lakers to the title. What's worse, he seemed to know it. He claimed, "I trust the team. I just trust myself more."[16] But this is the opposite of what engaging leaders do; they trust the team first. Bryant needed to learn that.

Horace Grant saw this in his years with Michael Jordan. Grant knew Jackson taught Jordan to reach out to his teammates to build trust. Bryant had to do the same thing, even if it didn't come naturally. Grant noted, "To be a leader, everybody has to respect you on and off the court. You can't just be a great player. Every once in a while, you have to be able to say, 'I made a mistake. My fault.'"[17]

Ego caused big problems on the Seattle Mariners, but the team was able to overcome them. Ken Griffey, Jr. was considered by many to be the best all-around player in baseball during the 1990s. As long as he was smiling and helping lead the team, it was successful, winning division titles in 1995 and 1997. Then things began to happen. The team got off to a slow start in 1998 because of injuries, and star pitcher Randy Johnson was traded during the season when the team thought he would cost too much to re-sign in 1999. Griffey started worrying about his own future and whether the team was committed to winning. He lost his focus on the team and his trust in leadership to fix things.

Junior was scheduled to become a free agent after the 1999 season, and speculation swirled around him all year. By the middle of the season, Griffey went into a funk. His mood was bad and detracted from the team, his contract was not resolved, and the M's moved into a new ballpark, Safeco Field, which was a pitcher's park. Their old stadium, the Kingdome, had been hitter-friendly. Junior's production fell way off, he got surly, and the team couldn't recover, finishing third in a four-team division.

At the end of the season, the team tried to re-sign Griffey, but he wanted out of Seattle to return home to Cincinnati. He used his leverage to force a trade, even accepting below-market money from the Reds to go home. Most baseball experts thought the M's didn't get much in return, just a journeyman pitcher, a pretty good center-fielder to replace Griffey, and two prospects. They predicted the demise of the Mariners without their star.

But General Manager Pat Gillick proved to be very shrewd when he let Johnson and Griffey go. For Johnson in 1998, he received two good young pitchers and a shortstop who blossomed during 2000 and 2001. He used the money he saved by not re-signing Griffey to get three free agent pitchers, two infielders, and another outfielder, none of whom were hugely expensive. Now the M's had a completely new mix of talent, heavy on pitching and defense that was better suited for their big new ballpark.

The reinvented team jelled under Lou Piniella. The chemistry was great and there were no distracting personality conflicts, despite star Alex Rodriquez playing out his contract. "We've got a nice combination of personalities," said outfielder Jay Buhner.[18] The Mariners won the wild card spot to get into the 2000 AL playoffs. The two pitchers obtained for Johnson started against the White Sox in the first two games of the playoff series, and the M's swept the Sox in three games. They went on to the AL Championship Series where they gave the Yankees a tough fight before losing.

NO MORE COMMAND, CONTROL, AND CONSTANT CRITICISM

Another enemy of trust is old style command-and-control leadership. Usually, this is accompanied by constant criticism. Sometimes it's part of micromanaging. Command, control, and criticism helped cause the failures of Mike Ditka in New Orleans and Rick Pitino in Boston. Skilled people won't put up with it anymore. You can't be too nice—people want leaders to be strong, principled, and courageous. But you can't be too critical and commanding because talented people will hit the street.

A command-and-control-style leader hasn't won a single major sports championship in recent years. The leaders have either been builders who got tough when he needed to or drivers who toned it down as required.

The most successful coach in the history of professional hockey is recently retired Scotty Bowman. Bowman started coaching in the NHL in 1967, won more games than any other coach, and captured nine Stanley Cups—five in Montreal, one in Pittsburgh, and three in Detroit. He achieved that success by changing with the times. Philadelphia Coach Ken Hitchcock said, "Most people of his status, like Woody Hayes and Bobby Knight, who have won on a consistent basis with old-school techniques, have not adjusted to new school personalities. Scotty has kept the same ideas and principles, but he has adjusted to the times."[19]

The soap opera in Philadelphia during the 76ers' breakthrough 2000–2001 season shows just how hard it is for some leaders to change. This was no secret. Larry Brown publicly acknowledged several times that he needed to be more careful and upbeat about what he said and did. Brown went out of his way to praise Iverson and the team, rather than criticize, and be a more open and positive leader.

Still, Brown was stressed-out from trying to change. During December of 2000, he blew up at the team after a bad game and then realized he needed to take a few days off to regroup. It's extraordinarily rare when a pro coach takes a few days off from his team. Then Sixers' forward George Lynch said, "This team isn't good at talking to each other when we need to talk to each other. You let it build up, then all of a sudden you have a blowup. It's one of those things where Coach Brown needed a break from us, and we probably needed a break from him."[20] When Brown came back, he said again he needed to be more positive and trusting.

One coach who hasn't been able to make the change is Pat Riley. He tries from time to time, but it doesn't seem to stick. Before the 2001 season, Riley vowed he would loosen his control, provide more freedom, and be less critical. But it didn't last. Ricky Davis, a young player Riley traded away very early in the year said, "I saw a few changes, but you can't keep bad habits away, like working guys too hard, not letting you be yourself. It's back to the same old, same old. There's such a thing as constructive criticism."[21]

Engaging leaders have to initiate contact and build relationships in a trusting, positive way. You may want your people to commit to your goals, but they won't unless you trust them first.

SUPERB COMMUNICATIONS

You need to become a superb, frequent, and honest communicator to capture and keep the trust of your employees. That's one reason broadcasters are moving directly from announcing to managing. They hone their communication skills in the booth and then transfer them to their leadership roles. Larry Dierker made the jump and enjoyed a successful career with the Houston Astros, leading them to the NL Central title four out of the five years he managed them. Unfortunately, he never could get the team past the first round of the playoffs. That got him fired after 2001. Ironically, for a former broadcaster, he also hurt his cause by being too curt in his post-game interviews after the Astros lost big games.

Bob Brenly was incredibly successful right away. A long-time broadcaster with just a little coaching experience, Brenly went directly from the booth to the field, managing the Diamondbacks and winning the World Series in his first year. There he faced off against Joe Torre, who had a losing record for 14 years as a manager before becoming a broadcaster himself. Torre went from announcing to managing the Yankees, where he fixed his won-lost record.

Brenly's a builder, a free spirit, and a risk taker, in the style of his mentor, Dusty Baker. "I learned a lot from Dusty, the way he handled his ball clubs there," Brenly says. "He does a lot by his hunches and gut feelings and lives with it. I think players appreciate it a lot more than if you just sit there and go by the numbers."[22] He supports, even cheerleads for his players. In the World Series, when he needed to go to the mound to pull Curt Schilling who didn't want to come out, Benly took the ball and proclaimed loudly, "You're my hero." How could Schilling argue?

Players describe Brenly as very emotional and usually very positive. Slugger Luis Gonzalez said, "He's the first guy at the top of the steps cheering for guys when they do well. That's the way he played. He gets very emotional when something positive happens, and that fires us up as players."[23] However, his passion and skill at communicating also led him to do some judicious screaming on occasion. According to Brenly, "They [the players] just need a little push in the right direction from time to time."

Another broadcaster-turned-coach is Doc Rivers, a long-time NBA player who became a television analyst when he retired from playing. From there he was hired to coach the Orlando Magic in 1999. Rivers had no coaching experience and no star players, but he was an instant success, winning coach of the year honors in his first season.

Maybe the strongest endorsement of Rivers came from his players. In their next-to-last game of the season, the Magic lost and was eliminated from the playoffs. With nothing at stake but pride in its last game, the team pulled together and won for Doc. When it was over, every player said he couldn't wait to come back and play for Rivers again. People who watched Rivers said he succeeded because he was a great salesman. He pitched his agenda to his players with great enthusiasm. In addition, he listened, learned, and kept adapting his approach to fit his team. More than just sales skills, these are the communication skills of an engaging leader.

ALL YOU NEED IS LOVE

Trust is the foundation of performance. Trust means people will think you're a fair person and buy in to what you're trying to do. But they won't necessarily run through walls for you. Trust is just the start. You've got to go further.

If trust gets you to good, appreciation gets you to great. William James, the father of American psychology, said appreciation is the deepest principle in human nature. In the words of Dick Vermeil, "Be a hugger."[24]

Some recent research looked at management behaviors across many different studies and companies. The conclusion was that a "female" style of leadership works best today.[25] Our most engaging leaders now show caring, listening, and public expressions of positive emotions, along with a deeper understanding and acknowledgement of how others are feeling. These are Dick Vermeil's "huggers." They show their appreciation.

A big company recently asked me to help it become a great employer. That was one of its goals. When I got there, I saw the opposite. The company had good financial performance and pretty good customer satisfaction for its industry, but employees thought it was a cold and distant place—probably the reason customer service was just OK. Formal dress was still the rule, and men kept their suit coats on all the time. A rigid hierarchy was still in place, both in the organization and in the way people behaved toward each other. Employees were expected to address their superiors by Mr., Mrs., or Miss. Just as importantly, employees didn't see much collaboration across departments or extra effort by coworkers.

The company asked me to speak to top management at a leadership meeting at a resort. Despite the location, the group continued to be dressed formally. I told them the missing element in their company was warmth. To be a great employer, they had to loosen up and warm up the place. I told them what Dick Vermeil said. Then I asked each of the 150 top executives to take off their coats, loosen their ties, and hug the person next to them. They did it, but very, very reluctantly. You would have thought I was making them take bad tasting medicine. As you can imagine, this was the last time I spoke to that group.

My request wasn't so far-fetched. Winning teams in sports and business always talk about themselves as "families." No less an authoritarian than the late Vince Lombardi said that *teams don't win until the players love each other.*[26]

Brian Billick said he learned this from his Super Bowl winning Ravens. "This team taught me what the concept of team is about. The terms *team* and *family* are interchangeable. When you go through what this team has gone through this last year, the sense of family does come through."[27]

Maybe you're not a hugger, but you can still show appreciation. Saying thank you gets things started. How often do you thank your employees for their work, even when it's something they're supposed to do?

Public and private recognition works well too. Everyone loves to be praised. When I'm coaching executives, a problem I often discover is that they're just not positive enough with their people. They take good works for granted. You can't build a productive atmosphere for professionals without being positive. A simple technique I use to increase the amount of praise they give is to ask them to carry a 3" × 5" card and make a tic mark every time they say something nice to someone. You'd be amazed at how fast their praise goes up and how fast people notice it. Employees talk about it right away. They thank their leaders for saying thanks. Moreover, the buzz is so strong that these executives start doing it at home and immediately create happier spouses and children.

At the root of appreciation is showing people you care about their opinions. I'll never forget what one alienated professional told me about how his organization should engage him and his peers. It was so simple and yet so powerful. He said, "Listen to us, value us, take us seriously." Listening seriously to someone is the start of appreciation.

When you show appreciation on a regular basis, you're able to turn up the intensity or make big changes when needed. Sometimes that's lighting a fire under people. After the Lakers dropped the first game of the 2001 NBA Finals to Philadelphia, Phil Jackson needed Shaquille O'Neal to play a lot harder. Just before the next game started, Jackson chided Shaq, "Don't be afraid to block a shot tonight."[28] O'Neal stopped and stared at his coach. Then he took that energy into the game and blocked eight shots, a championship series record, to lead the Lakers to the win.

Sometimes you can increase the intensity by turning down the heat. If you're loud all the time, silence can be deafening. This is what Jim O'Brien did when he took over from Rick Pitino in mid-season as coach of the Boston Celtics. The Celtics were 12–22 in 2000–2001 and 99–147 overall under Pitino who tried, with little success, to coach pros like they were college players. Pitino was constantly up from the sidelines yelling and glaring at his players, trying to control them through what he thought was teaching. His players thought he was just screaming at them and trying to direct their every move. They tuned him out.

The NBA is a player's league, and the players saw Pitino as a distraction—someone who would criticize them publicly while keeping the attention for himself. "Because of the way things were, very negative, the first two months of the season, the focus wasn't on us," said star forward Antoine Walker after Pitino left. "It was obviously on coach Pitino and whatever he was going to do with his career. Now, the focus is on us and the guys are just going out there and playing hard and giving it everything we got."[29]

O'Brien changed everything by turning the attention on the players—easy for him to do because he's a low-key guy—letting them play, and praising them publicly whenever he got the chance. "No matter who's on the sidelines, it comes down to the players getting the job done all four quarters. They have got to get the stops. In the fourth quarter, we're going to put the ball in their hands, Antoine Walker and Paul Pierce. You can talk about coaching styles, but they have got to get the job done," said O'Brien.[30]

His methods worked as the Celtics went on a winning streak and competed for a playoff spot, losing out in the last days. The next year they made the playoffs and went all the way to the Eastern Conference finals. Ironically, the Celtics became a much better defensive team with O'Brien as coach, even though defense was Pitino's focus. By laying back, O'Brien was able to get the players to work harder on defense, which in basketball is mostly effort and teamwork. "Everybody's playing with a lot of confidence and believing in each other," said Walker. "That's a credit to coach O'Brien."[31]

Failure to appreciate is another thing that tripped Pitino in Boston. He had the power to pick his team, and he made several bad draft choices and trades. Then he compounded his mistakes by saying publicly he wouldn't have taken the Celtics job if he'd known he wasn't going to get Tim Duncan in the NBA draft. This insulted his current players who felt unappreciated. They were more than happy to point their fingers at him after he left, even after he signed them to big contracts. Said guard Randy Brown, "A month ago [with Pitino], we lose this game by 30 points. . . . We would have been bickering, finger-pointing, second-guessing, all that stuff.

Right now, we're much looser and we're playing with confidence. I wonder why."[32]

NO APPRECIATION, NO TALENT

People perform best when they feel appreciated. People talk all the time, so a leader's reputation as a boss who shows appreciation gets around. Employees say a company's reputation as a good employer is very important to whether they'll come to work or stay there. Likewise, your reputation as an appreciative supervisor helps determine whether people want to work for you. News spreads fast. *If you don't show appreciation, the best people won't come work for you.*

Nowhere has this been truer than with the Chicago Bulls. With Phil Jackson, Michael Jordan, and company, the team won six NBA titles during the 1990s. General manager Jerry Krause never thought he got the credit he deserved for building the team around Jordan. Jordan was so great, many people thought he could have won those titles with four guys from the local gym. Krause seethed from this lack of recognition and never gave any good feeling in return.

Instead, Krause coined the phrase "players don't win championships, organizations win championships."[33] Jordan took this as an insult to him and his teammates. He turned it around and used it to poke fun at Krause, and their relationship completely deteriorated.

It was no better with Jackson. Krause thought Jackson owed him complete loyalty because he hired him from the CBA as an assistant coach and then promoted him to head coach. As Jackson became more successful, he became more independent of Krause and increased Krause's distance from the players. Krause hated this so much that Jackson was the only member of Bulls management not invited to Krause's daughter's wedding.

All this bitterness wore everyone down. Krause threatened to get rid of Jackson, but Jordan said he wouldn't play for anyone but Phil. Without Jackson, there would be no Jordan and no title. Phil had the leverage, but the bad feelings grew.

After the fifth championship, Jackson agreed to come back for one more year, the "last dance" as he called it. Krause wanted to make sure Phil wouldn't reconsider. At the press conference announcing Jackson's contract, Krause said publicly it would be the last. Then he leaned over to Phil and said, "I don't care if you go 82–0, you're out of here."[34] After the sixth title, Jackson, Jordan, Scottie Pippen, Dennis Rodman, and other key players scattered, leaving the team in shambles.

As the old saying goes, be careful what you wish for because you may get it. Krause got his. He desperately wanted to build a winning team without Jordan so he could finally get his due. He stockpiled his cash and high draft picks to sign top-tier free agents and great rookies to rebuild. But his dreams were dashed. By the 2000–2001 season, the Bulls were by far the worst team in basketball, with about half the number of wins as the next worse team and little hope in sight.

Krause's main weapon, his cash horde, did him no good. The NBA approved a new collective bargaining agreement designed to put in an orderly salary structure. Players' financial opportunities were limited by their years of service and existing teams had equal chances of re-signing their best players to produce more fan loyalty. In some ways, the impact of the structure made it more like pay practices in the rest of business where companies can't wildly overspend for talent or they'll go broke. Instead, teams had to recruit free agents not only with money but also with the type of environment they could offer.

Krause had more money to spend than anyone after the 1999–2000 season, but he couldn't sign great players. Players remembered how he treated Jordan and the others and stayed away. Krause could only attract lesser talents and he was the only one bidding for them. This continued the following year. Again Krause had the money. Again all he could attract were the lesser lights among free agents.

The players knew the score. Minnesota all-star Kevin Garnett said, "It wasn't like somebody dropped a bomb and all of a sudden they went from classy to ashy. The management there totally made all those decisions in which to go and the direction they wanted to go in."[35]

Dallas all-star Michael Finley added, "I've met Jerry two times, once when I played Michael Jordan in one-on-one and he kicked me out of the gym and the second time when I worked out for the Bulls. He would have treated me better the second time if he had drafted me. But he didn't."[36]

More savvy management also understood. Atlanta Hawks general manager Pete Babcock said, "The reality in today's NBA is that players talk, and the way your own players feel about your organization is the message that's getting sent out."[37]

Mark Cuban bought the Dallas Mavericks in 2000. He made his money in the dot-com world and may understand our talent-based economy better than anyone in the league. When asked about re-signing Finley, Cuban replied, "Making Michael Finley happy on a day-to-day basis before we get to the off-season is my goal. When it comes down to time to sign him, it's already too late. If we don't communicate now with Mike to know what his goals and desires are and how he wants to be treated, it'll be too late."[38] Cuban had no trouble resigning Finley.

That's what you need to do as a leader in this economy. Know and understand the needs and goals of your most talented people because they are absolutely crucial to retain. Demonstrate appreciation to everyone on your team because everyone has a role to play. If people can't do what you need them to do, get rid of them and make room for others who can. When you show appreciation and build strong relationships, you can push people to the heights of performance. And they'll deliver. Huggers win Super Bowls.

THE HUDDLE

If you're a builder:

- You're good at extending trust, but don't feel hurt if someone you trust doesn't come through for you. It's probably not personal.

- Don't confuse liking someone with performance. You must lead and make decisions based on performance, not how much you like someone or how you want him or her to feel about you. Dependability and reliability—your's and others'—are essential for nurturing trust on your team.

- You're good at not micromanaging, but don't become too lax. You must hold people accountable for results, and you must follow up. This will increase trust and good feeling, not detract from them.

- Do whatever you can to promote strong peer relationships on your team. Yet when there's a dispute or egos clash, lay down the law. Take corrective action as soon as you recognize the problem.

- Show your appreciation for performance.

If you're a driver:

- Work harder at extending trust. If someone fails you, don't generalize that failure to others. Keep trying with other people.

- Stick with your people even if they make a few mistakes or hit a little slump. If they performed before, they'll perform again—especially if you give them some extra support, listening, and a vote of confidence.

- You're likely to micromanage. Stop it. Set demanding goals and standards but let people do their work. Show them you trust them to perform.

- Do whatever you can to promote strong peer relationships on your team. Let people's egos come out a bit. Help people relax, be themselves, and relate to each other without you in the middle.

- Show your appreciation for who they are.

CHAPTER SEVEN

CHEMISTRY

Structure

"Why didn't you hit a home run like I told you to? If you're
not going to do what I tell you, what's the use of
my being manager?"

—Groucho Marx, managing a celebrity softball team, to one of his players

THE STRUCTURE OF ENGAGEMENT

Think of chemistry as a car you want to drive. Structure is the engine that motors you to your goals. Trust is the fuel that powers the engine. Chemistry is the car because cars, like team chemistry, are more than the sum of their parts. Cars have psychological and social aspects to them, just like team chemistry. You need enough car, and enough chemistry, to get you where you want to go. Sometimes you'll go in grand style; other times you'll just barely make it or break down.

Like fuel, trust enables you to power the structure you want to implement. This car analogy breaks down, however, because usually the more successful you become, the more trust you generate. We'd all love it if gasoline would regenerate as we get closer to our destinations—well, maybe the oil companies wouldn't. With more trust, more people will buy into your plan.

At its most basic, structure is about designing what tasks need to be done, creating jobs to do them, and assigning them to people. When people do their jobs dependably and that leads to success, structure contributes to chemistry. Your organization structure depends on the work you're doing, your business strategy, operating model, underlying systems, and size and customer requirements, among other things. That's a lot to consider, and it would take a whole book to do it, so I'm not going to try. Instead, I'm going to discuss *the four elements of structure that impact most on becoming an engaging leader: accountability, execution, roles, and rewards.*

Sports shines a light on engaging people through structure because, as I said earlier, the success models in each sport are pretty much the same and haven't changed in years. The infinite variety of ways to succeed that exists in business doesn't exist in sports. Stout defense with just enough offense wins in baseball, basketball, hockey, and football, unless you're the Rams. So, structure varies by the personal preferences of the leader and the talent he or she has.

That's why I'm always fascinated to see coaches in the same sport take very different approaches to structuring their teams. It reveals so much about what they think they need to do to engage people to win. We learn from them whether they're right or wrong.

It's well accepted now that your organization should be as flat as possible. De-layering takes out costs, increases speed of decision making, promotes communication, and enables more entrepreneurial behavior. Excess hierarchy leads to unnecessary bureaucracy. In addition, it conflicts with the values of baby boomers and the generations that followed. These people increasingly prize meritocracy and self-direction, so you need to justify every bit of hierarchy you have. If you don't, it seems like phony power or status and extra cost and distance. Simply put, we have millions of people now who question authority. It isn't just Allen Iverson.

For this reason, pay attention to these three principles as you organize for engagement:

1. *Self-organization.* The more you support people in creating their own organizations—whether these are teams, networks, alliances, processes, etc.—the more they'll feel in charge of their futures. When you dictate both the form and functions of your organization, you take away self-control. High-performing organizations encourage more self-control than system control. Again, the absolute amount of self-control you can allow depends on the work you do—it's a lot different for a research scientist than it is for a pilot or a nurse. But the more, the better. You'll know you went too far when you lose consistency or make too many unforced errors.

2. *Affinity.* Left to their own devices, people will associate and communicate with people whom they like and are like them. We see this in the clubhouse or locker room, when pitchers hang out with other pitchers, Spanish-speaking players hang out with other Spanish speakers, and offensive lineman communicate with each other in a language only they can understand. This isn't a bad thing. Engaging leaders use this to their advantage by building on natural affinities to create strong bonds. You can even challenge these subgroups to rise to new levels of performance or take on a special assignment, and they will based on bonding. But you have to make sure these groups integrate with each other. In high-performing organizations, subsystems talk to each other. If you lose that, you just have a bunch of cliques.

3. *Loose-tight.* Whatever structure you create, leave room for freedom inside it. The more structure you create, the more

freedom you should have. Ideally, you should build a structure that enables you to manage flexibility. Then you can really master change. This is what Phil Jackson says he loves about the triangle offense in basketball. It's a highly systematized way to create free-flowing shooting opportunities for players. In some types of businesses, you can structure your organization on values and leave room for individual decision making within those values. In others, you may have tight process control over service delivery or production but establish other paths for people to suggest ways to change and improve basic processes. High-performing organizations balance structure and freedom.

ACCOUNTABILITY—DON'T GET TOO COMFORTABLE

In the short-term world of business and sports, you have to win right away. Accountability for instant success is everywhere (unless you coach the Chicago Bulls). Pat Burns, a three-time NHL coach of the year, found that out.

Burns, the coach of the Boston Bruins, was fired just eight games into the 2000–2001 hockey season. The Bruins missed the playoffs the year before, so Burns was on a short leash. Boston started by winning three and tying one of its first four games. Then it went on a western road trip and lost all four games. That was the end of Burns. Mike Keenan, the ultimate "win at all costs" coach and an intimidating driver, replaced him.

Keenan had coached many teams in the league and was successful at all his stops. He also developed a well-deserved reputation for fighting with team executives for more power. Seeing what was coming, Harry Sinden, the long-time president of the Bruins, retired the next week. Keenan's Bruins didn't make the playoffs either, and, appropriately enough, he was fired immediately after the season.

Fifteen games into the 2000–2001 NBA season, with a record of six wins and nine losses, the Seattle SuperSonics fired Coach Paul Westphal. Westphal had a successful history as a pro coach, leading the Phoenix Suns to the NBA finals in 1993 and the Sonics into the playoffs in 1999–2000. However, the team got off to a poor start amid internal fighting and insubordination.

Westphal actually offered to resign after four games, but the team refused him. During the 12th game of the season, the coach got into an on-court argument with star guard Gary Payton and suspended him. The team president, Wally Walker, retracted the suspension after Payton apologized. Usurped and under attack, the Sonics let Westphal out of his misery a week later.[1]

Stories like this go on and on, and not just in sports. CEO turnover is at an all-time high, despite a shortage of people to fill those jobs. There even may be a shortage of people who want those jobs. Just one year after taking over Coca-Cola and instituting huge changes to get the soft drink giant back in a growth mode, Chairman and CEO Douglas Daft found himself the subject of a *Business Week* story[2] questioning whether he was changing enough things as quickly as necessary. With pressure like this, you have to be extraordinarily strong-willed just to aspire to leadership.

It's not just leaders who are under this intense pressure; everyone feels it. For 13 years, Mark Grace played first base for the Cubs. Though he didn't hit with much power, he had more hits than anyone in baseball during the 1990s and was a terrific fielder. Grace loved the Cubs and the fans loved Grace. Still, after the Cubs had two more dismal seasons in 1999 and 2000, the team decided it needed someone else. It also didn't want to pay Grace what he would have commanded to stay in Chicago for 2001.

Of course, the move backfired on the Cubs. They struggled at first base all year and were forced to trade for Fred McGriff, who cost a lot more than Grace. Grace went on to have a solid year for Arizona and starred in the World Series. He got the first hit in the bottom of the 9th inning of game seven to start the Diamondbacks' victory rally.

Things like this happen all the time in sports; that's why athletes have such good unions. Another Chicago athlete, former Bears defensive tackle Mike Wells, summed it up nicely when he quoted what one of his coaches told the team, "You will be tolerated as long as it takes to replace you." Wells said, "They're always looking to replace everybody. It would be silly to ever get comfortable."[3] After a few good seasons with the Bears, Wells was replaced too.

There's no evidence this kind of fear motivates large numbers of employees. It sure hasn't helped the Bears or Cubs for most of the last century. Employees are no different than highly paid athletes in this regard. *Your people need to feel some level of personal security,* especially with all the pressure on them to perform. The most engaging leaders demonstrate that mistakes are for learning, not for punishing or avoiding. Once you start penalizing people for mistakes or managing them so they don't take risks, you drive innovation out of your business. That's a huge blunder.

On the other hand, you can't allow mistakes to keep recurring. Nor can you allow discipline to slip. When it comes to setting accountabilities and executing against them, engaging leaders:

- Set a clear direction—your big goal

- Break the goal down into measurable results and then set performance targets at excellence to get stretch results

- Assign individual or team accountabilities for these results

- Push hard to get the needed outcomes and reward success as you get them

- Maintain firm discipline that sets an example so people learn to discipline themselves

- Ease up as people show they're meeting your standards

This instills the toughness in teams and people that winning requires. It works in all performance endeavors, business as well as sports, though how heavy-handed you can be in the way you do it depends on the business you're leading. In professional services and other places with highly paid knowledge workers, you have to take a lighter approach or your intellectual capital will walk out the door. In manufacturing, sales, and distribution businesses, successful CEOs often insist on more conformity and are quicker to address people who don't toe the line, though they can't get away with the way they managed ten years ago.

EXECUTE WITH EXCELLENCE

Executing with excellence takes three things: appropriate discipline, attention to the right details, and a simple plan. These are the basics. *Winning requires you to be world class at doing the basics.* When you're not, you won't meet your goals and standards.

Stay Disciplined

Larry Robinson turned around the New Jersey Devils and led them to the 2000 Stanley Cup by instilling a stronger sense of order and teamwork. Scott Stevens, the team captain, said, "The biggest thing Larry brought is discipline. He got everyone playing as a team, not individuals."[4]

Robinson approached this in a calm, building style and the immediacy of the playoffs created urgency to right things quickly. He ran tough practices and focused on winning through outstanding defense. He worked with players individually, helping them focus on their strengths. These methods earned everyone's trust. However, when the situation called for it, Robinson raised his voice to previously unheard volumes.

During a crucial loss in the Eastern Conference finals, Robinson saw the team "dogging it," playing lazily and letting victory slip away. In the locker-room after the game, the mild-mannered Robinson started screaming so loudly people could hear him across the building. "It was just something I felt had to be done. I would've hated to have that series end knowing they had not given their best," said Robinson.[5]

Apparently it worked. The players described it as "shocking but effective," and they went on to win the Cup.

This is a great example of appropriate discipline, especially for a builder—setting the tone and enforcing rules with composure and intensity, while letting loose with genuine anger when people cross critical boundaries. Of course, the emotion should be celebration when things go right, just as easily as it could be scolding when things go wrong. People respect genuine displays of feeling as long as you're not constantly criticizing them or flashing your ego. If you do that, people will tune you out.

It is possible to keep your emotions at a high pitch all the time and be a successful leader, but it's much harder to do. The few executives I've seen succeed with this style show far more raging enthusiasm and love than disparagement or disapproval. This allows them to be critical when they need to be. But most people aren't built this way. The natural tendency for more people seems to be quieter or more negative, with not enough caring and optimism. Negativity discourages people and saps their motivation.

Details, Details, Details

Attention to details is the second part of proper execution, as well as a characteristic of outstanding leadership. Even "big picture" leaders have to watch the details. If they don't, details will destroy them. Which details you attend to is a function of the system or model you use to run your business. *Don't micromanage, delegate. But keep a close eye on what counts.*

Bill Belichick led the surprising New England Patriots to the Super Bowl with a fanatical eye on defensive details. His team entered the game as huge underdogs to the offensive juggernaut known as the St. Louis Rams. It emerged victorious by doing what very few teams had done all season, stopping the Rams score-at-will offense.

Belichick has a huge reputation as a defensive genius, built on a foundation of creativity and detailed preparation. He programs defensive schemes the way most teams diagram offensive plays. He shows opposing offenses vastly different looks depending on how the offense lines up, trying to confuse them. His teams learn many more defenses per game than most football teams to achieve his goal of disrupting the competition.

Yet through all of this complexity, Belichick keeps simplicity and focus uppermost. "You have to have enough so you can counter your opponent, but keep it simple enough so your players can execute."[6] After putting in all these plays, Belichick then "compresses" them by grouping them and making them easy to remember. One of his players, Terrell Buckley, said, "It's a common sense defense that uses lots of groupings, and they get it across and make you feel like it's not on you but you are involved. We get to suggest things. We retain it."[7]

Contrast this with the playbook Miami Heat players get every year from Pat Riley. Before the 2000–2001 season Riley presented his team with a 257-page-playbook—in a league where some teams don't even have one. It's so big, some of the players couldn't understand or remember it. A star player, Eddie Jones, said, "I've had some textbooks that long in college. But I don't think the ones [playbooks] I've had every year could amount to that."[8] It didn't help much. The Heat flamed out early in the playoffs that year. Details for details' sake just weigh too heavily on people. Figure out what your critical success factors are, pay close attention to them and do what it takes to get your team to execute them. Leave the minutiae alone to be handled by others.

Keep It Simple

The last part of execution is simplicity. Simple is best. When Jim O'Brien took over the Celtics and started them winning, he made things easier on the players. One of his star players, Paul Pierce, said, "He simplified our scheme. He's not playing as many people as before, he's not pressing as much, and sticks to one game plan. That makes us execute better rotations because we keep fewer things in mind."[9]

The Utah Jazz has taken this philosophy to extremes—with tremendous success. Jerry Sloan has run the same, simple pick-and-roll offense since he took over as coach in 1988. The pick-and-roll is a basketball play you teach kids in junior high school. Using this constant scheme and strong defense, Sloan has won nearly 64 percent of his games and made the playoffs every year. He reached the NBA finals in 1997 and 1998, only to lose to Michael Jordan and the Bulls.

Sloan has the longest tenure with the same team of any coach in any pro sport. Because the NBA averages more than ten coaching changes a year, this is more than remarkable. It's also a tribute to how simplicity and consistency enables you to execute superbly and win.

It helps Sloan and Utah that the cornerstones of the team, Karl Malone and John Stockton, have been together since 1985. *Continuity makes everything easier.* That's why a leader who churns personnel has so much difficulty getting people to execute consistently. Stockton is the NBA's all-time assists leader, and he starts the pick-and-roll on offense. Usually, the ball ends up with Malone, who has become the second leading scorer in NBA history by completing the play for a basket. One reason the Jazz have this consistency is because Malone and Stockton love playing for Sloan.

On the other hand, trying to do too much almost always gets you in trouble. The Cleveland Browns and Chicago Bears suffered from the same disease of trying to do too much on offense during the 2000 season. Coaches Chris Palmer of the Browns and Dick Jauron of the Bears both came from the Jacksonville Jaguars who ran a complex passing scheme. The scheme depended on the quarterback and the receivers making adjustments while they ran their routes, depending on how the receivers were covered by the defense. The Jags had enough good talent at quarterback and wide receiver to make it work for a while. The Browns and Bears put in similar plans, but neither team had the players to execute this scheme and lost most of their games.

Palmer was fired after the 2000 season. His replacement, Butch Davis, brought in a new offensive coordinator whose first pronouncement was, "The Browns' offense will be going from French to Spanish."[10] He was trying to say his receivers were going to have defined routes, instead of choices to make while the play was happening. This simplified and improved the offense.

Fortunately, the Bears came to the same conclusion. Near the end of another disastrous season, the offensive coordinator left, much to the relief of Bears' players and fans. His replacement also simplified the passing schemes and the Bears improved right away

Superior execution starts with a simple plan that you keep trying to outperform. As one of my clients likes to say, "Success means never being satisfied." Keep it simple and stay hungry to do better.

ROLES: SHINING STARS

Face it, not everyone on your team is a star. There are only so many Michael Jordans or Derek Jeters. This doesn't diminish your team or you. It doesn't mean you're less effective as a builder or a driver. No matter how carefully you select or how skillfully you develop people, they will perform differently at various times.

You are far better off if your team is comprised of the necessary number of stars and complementary role players who know their jobs, do them well, and step up their performance from time to time. You can tailor your performance demands and your development plans accordingly. Your stars are the 10 to 20 percent who really shine, and your role players are the other 70 to 80 percent who are solid citizens. Just make sure the 10 percent at the bottom don't drag people down with them. As Casey Stengel said, "The secret of managing is to keep the guys who hate you away from the guys who are undecided."[11]

It's pretty clear that the great teams of the last several years had the requisite number of stars—two or three in basketball, six to eight in baseball, and 12 to 15 in football—supported by very competent teammates. If your stars are up to the challenge, and if one of them is a great closer, this is a winning formula and a great way to think about the roles on your team.

Leading this way requires you to:

- Build the right relationships with the right stars and expect them to be peer leaders

- Get rid of a star that doesn't fit the position or get him or her out of the leader's role

- Make sure everyone knows their roles and accountabilities and embraces them

- Get rid of people who won't accept their roles

People crave role clarity, and engaging leaders provide it. At the same time, if someone only wants to perform to the limits of his or her role and won't reach out to accept other responsibilities, that's a danger sign. This person probably is of limited use because you have to continually upgrade your team's performance. You need people who accept the ambiguity that goes with doing business and will raise their efforts to meet increased demands. This is a sign they're fully engaged.

You also need the stars on your team to be peer leaders. Peer leaders set the example for your team regarding work ethic, taking direction, pushing for excellence, remaining calm under pressure, and getting things done. With an effective peer leader, you can communicate your goals, set standards, get buy-in, and execute. They also help you build trust and chemistry.

Larry Brown believed Allan Iverson's emergence as the team leader was why the Sixers became the best team in the NBA's Eastern Conference in 2000–2001. "He's accepted his responsibility. That's the only way a coach can succeed in this league—if your best players set the standards."[12] Your stars help set the tone for whether others will follow you. If you don't have that kind of peer leader, you had better get one.

Brown probably went a bit too far in his description. You have to set the standards, but if you can do that together with your stars, you'll get higher performance. When they're not interested in that, you'll lose.

Shaquille O'Neal knew this too. During the Lakers' troubles in 2000–2001, he said, "You can't be a good leader if you don't have good listeners."[13] O'Neal was frustrated trying to get Kobe Bryant to play Phil Jackson's system. To O'Neal, Bryant was a "lone ranger" who didn't want to follow and had a destructive impact on the team.

Some critics felt Cubs' star Sammy Sosa seemed more interested in his own statistics, fame, and contract than leading the team to victory in 1999 and 2000. It didn't help Don Baylor to start his tenure as Cubs manager in 2000 by insulting Sosa's fielding. Sosa's very proud and thought Baylor was blaming him for the Cubs' problems. He didn't help Baylor assume team leadership, and by 2002 Baylor was fired.

If your star performer isn't the right type of leader, you're in trouble. This was the Seattle SuperSonics' problem in 2000–2001. Despite a change of coaches and a new approach, the volatile Gary Payton created problems for the team all season. Even with a lot of talent, the Sonics missed the playoffs in 2000–2001.

Nate McMillan, a friend and former teammate of Payton's, tried being positive when he took over for Paul Westphal. While Westphal was highly critical of some of the players—he spoke publicly of trading Payton and said coaching Vin Baker was like root canal[14]—McMillan took the opposite approach. When asked about trading Payton, McMillan said, "Why would you want to move a guy who is the top guard in the league? I know he loves Seattle and wants to be part of the organization."[15]

The players responded by going 38–29 under McMillan but there still were plenty of problems with Payton. McMillan suspended Payton after a fight with a teammate, and this time the team let it stick. Payton's behavior set the tone for the rest of the team and the in-fighting continued for most of the season. It didn't seem to ebb until the Sonics gave McMillan a four-year contract that established his authority. After that, even Payton seemed to settle down and take a more positive peer leadership role, at least for a while.

Your peer leaders have to be positive role models. If not, get rid of them. At the very least, move them out of leadership roles if you can. This isn't easy to do because whether it's your smartest engineer, most creative marketer, or strongest litigator, your team will suffer a short-term performance drop. Then it will reorganize around other people. In the long term, if you help the right people move into peer leader roles, you'll be able to impose your standards, other team members will become more positive, chemistry will improve, and results will increase.

Peer leaders arise on every team. You'd be hard pressed to reach long-term success without good ones. Find the right people and help them become peer leaders. It will enable you to engage everyone. As former baseball manager Sparky Anderson, who won World Series titles in both leagues, said when his team just traded for a new star player, "I just got a whole lot smarter."

WHAT DOES MONEY HAVE TO DO WITH IT?

There's no simple answer to how money affects talent and how you should use it to motivate and reward people. To some people, it's everything; to others, it's only one factor, although a very critical one, in where and how they choose to work. Former baseball owner Bill Veeck, who last owned a team at the beginning of the free agency era in baseball, thought it was all-important, probably because he never had very much of it. Once he was asked if free agents leaned toward playing in big cities. He replied, "Not really. They lean toward cash."[16]

Many years later Kendall Gill once again confirmed Veeck's judgement. Before the 2000–2001 season, the veteran guard/forward had a chance to sign with the Lakers and compete for a championship for $2.5 million, or stay with the losing New Jersey Nets for $7 million. "My ego was telling me championship, but in the end, I made a sound financial decision," said Gill.[17] Gill got his money, but the Lakers beat the Nets again. Gill played in only 31 games after suffering a knee injury early in the year.

On the other hand, some stars take less to play for a particular team. In 2001, Mark McGwire re-signed with the Cardinals for two years and $30 million, considered well below his market value, because he loved the fans, the team, and playing for Tony LaRussa. McGwire said, "I don't want to be anywhere else."[18] McGwire then retired halfway through the contract because he was hurt, couldn't perform up to his standards, and didn't want to take money he didn't deserve. Ken Griffey, Jr. also signed for less than market value to return to his hometown of Cincinnati and his beloved Reds.

Though you're unlikely to offer anyone $30 million for two years, here are some lessons about money and motivation as you try to engage talent in this mobile economy.

First, *understand what motivates people.* You can only do that by listening to them and hearing what's in their hearts. McGwire didn't even want to talk to other teams. Griffey had only one objective—to get back home. In contrast, Alex Rodriguez signed with the Texas Rangers in 2001, a bad team he had never considered joining, because they overwhelmed him with money.

Second, *remember everyone's different.* People do things for their own reasons, not for anyone else's; so pay attention to their reasons. Greed drives a lot of behavior, but so do other things. Stephon Marbury left the winning Timberwolves for the Nets for the same amount of money the T'Wolves offered. Marbury couldn't stand the thought of not being "the man" in Minnesota—the highest paid player. That designation would always belong to Kevin Garnett, whose $126 million contract led to the NBA lockout and new, reduced salary structure.

Third, listen to Bill Veeck. "It isn't the high price of stars that is expensive, it's the high price of mediocrity."[19] *Pay your stars a lot but don't overpay the rest.* Pay your best performers as much as you can. It won't hurt you; even Garnett's giant contract turned out to be a pretty good deal for his team because he's worth it. You get into trouble when you shell out too much for people who can't drive results.

No one yet has figured out a foolproof way to pay for performance, but several companies have figured out smart approaches. One of my favorites is a company that every year identifies its top 30 percent of employees. It makes sure these people are well paid and cared for and that they know it. If they hear someone in this 30 percent group is unhappy or looking around for a new job, they speak with the person right away about what's necessary to keep him or her. They simply try to stay market competitive with the other 70 percent. If these people get better offers, the company usually lets them go rather than overpay.

Fourth, *have somebody ready to take over* just in case you can't come to an agreement. Successful companies, like winning teams, almost always have somebody prepared and waiting to replace someone who wants to move on. Most of the best employers do their promoting from within the ranks. Engaging leaders make a heavy investment in and have effective processes for selection and development—the keys to talent management. Otherwise, you're always scrambling to plug holes, and that's no way to get ahead.

IT'S MONEY THAT MATTERS

There's an acronym in the compensation consulting business: GOOBER. It means Greed Obscures Other Believable Executive Rationale. After what we've seen with Enron, Tyco, WorldCom, and other companies, who could disagree? In fact, corporate executives and professional athletes like to use each other as justification for their high salaries. CEOs try to say their skills are unique, like pro stars, so they should be paid more or they can't do a good job. Of course, when you ask them if they'll work harder or smarter if you pay them more, they say they're already working as hard and as smart as they can. Athletes like to take the big money from their bosses, many of whom run or used to run corporations, and then say no one pays to watch the bosses play.

Financial largess only causes a problem when it gets in the way of winning. Alex Rodriquez signed the largest contract in baseball history with Texas before the 2001 season and his contract caused lots of problems for other teams. Maybe that was another plus for the Rangers. Surprisingly, nobody on the Rangers complained, probably figuring they'd get theirs some day.

Gary Sheffield of the Dodgers screamed loudly. He insisted it wasn't the money; of course, no one believed him. He wanted a big contract extension from the Dodgers or he wanted to be traded. Sheffield had a contract for three more years at $10 million a year, but with Rodriquez at $25 million, Sheffield thought he was getting cheated. Sheffield said, "It isn't about money, it's about the disrespect I've had to deal with since I came here."[20]

The Dodgers were astounded. They passed on chasing Rodriquez thinking Sheffield was happy—he had a fabulous year in 2000— and spent a lot of money on pitching instead. The Dodgers said they were in a state of shock over Sheffield and tried hard to move him. They wanted equal value, but other teams figured he wasn't worth the trouble. This wasn't the first time he'd acted out. Seattle Mariners' chairman Howard Lincoln called him "a mean-spirited man who has trouble understanding contractual obligation."[21]

Sheffield's act disrupted the Dodgers' spring training. Once he realized no one wanted him, he retracted his demands and apologized to the team.

Sheffield wasn't alone in whining over Rodriquez's money. White Sox star Frank Thomas, runner-up as AL MVP in 2000, also pouted and left camp in an ill-advised holdout. Thomas wanted long-term security, so in 1997 he signed a seven-year deal worth up to a possible $85 million with options and incentives. His salary for 2001 was "only" about $8 million, and he claimed he was "embarrassed" to be paid so little.[22]

Thomas's walkout was so ill conceived two of his veteran teammates tried to convince him to stay. Thomas didn't get his contract revised and came back to camp a few days later. In what may have been a first in sports, Thomas's agents resigned after the episode, saying they couldn't deal with someone like him.

Jealousy is part of human nature, but a big cause of these problems is that there doesn't seem to be much rhyme or reason to how
teams spend. Many companies do such a bad job of communicating
how and why they pay people, employees get jealous of one another, and I'm not talking about multimillion dollar salaries. Most
surveys suggest that less than half of employees think they're paid
appropriately for what they contribute to their companies. Less
than half also think their companies do a good job of explaining
how pay is determined.[23]

In fact, it's often not the amount of pay that bothers people but
how pay decisions are made and how little we know about them.
Think about golf. No one seems to complain about what golfers earn
because they're out there making it by themselves, based solely on
what they accomplish. Even those who get hefty endorsements,
corporate outings, and appearance fees only receive them because
of what they've achieved. It's pure pay for performance.

That's the secret of any good pay plan. But it's easier said than
done. Like your own golf game, you'll spend a lot of time trying to
get pay right, but it will never be perfect. Still, keep at it. Four more
things you should do to engage people through pay are:

1. *Don't overpay.* It'll put you out of business, or at least force
   you to get rid of people as a way of cutting costs. Some of
   these people likely will be ones you really need. Make sure
   you select for fit. That's key to getting outstanding performance in the first place.

2. *Avoid gross inequities in pay on your team.* Unless someone
   stands way above all the rest in performance, so much so
   that everyone else recognizes it, keep pay levels within a
   close range for similar responsibilities. Don't pay everyone

the same, but pay is no longer a secret; people talk about it all the time. If one person gets a lot more without being a much bigger contributor, you'll have problems.

3. *Explain your pay process.* Surveys repeatedly show people don't understand why they're paid what they're paid. This causes lots of dissatisfaction, even when people are happy with pay levels. This is one area where you can't communicate too much. Satisfaction with pay goes up with more communication about the pay process, even when you don't pay people more. Also, it's a lot cheaper than raising pay.

4. *Keep pay from being a distraction.* You want people to understand why they're getting what they're getting, but don't overemphasize it. If you do, you increase the chances that people will lose focus on what they're supposed to be doing. At times, companies raise pay issues when they don't have to, or even use pay as the main management tool. Then it's all anyone wants to think about.

WINNING OVER WHINING

In my experience, *a climate of trust and people of strong character win out over money* every time. Some companies feel if they pay everybody near the top of the market, then they shouldn't have to deal with the human side of the business. Leaders may think they're doing a great job if they fight hard to get every penny they can for their people and blame the company publicly if they don't get all they want. These companies and leaders are wrong.

You can win for years with average pay if you have strong leadership and chemistry. Powerful chemistry and good relationships will keep talented people who want to win. If you really engage them, people will go out of their way to perform because of their loyalty to you. If people want to work for you, they'll factor this into their thinking about whether to come to work or stay. This is a dollars-and-cents reason why your reputation as a leader and an employer is so crucial. You can determine how much your reputation is worth by how much it saves you in compensation.

A great example of this is the 2001 World Champion Diamondbacks. To bring a winner to Arizona quickly, owner Jerry Colangelo spent a lot of money on talent in the team's first years. The D'Backs won the NL West title in 1999, their second season, but fell to third place in 2000. Attendance dropped and cash flow became so tight Colangelo had to take out loans from baseball and do cash calls on his partners.

The players have genuine fondness for Colangelo and talk about what a great person he is to work for and be around. When Colangelo's financial problems mounted, he approached several players and asked for help in deferring large amounts of their salaries for 2001. Ten of the highest-paid players quickly agreed. "This is so far different from the norm," said Colangelo. "I think it goes back to the players we selected. We really did try to pick some people with character."[24] Pitcher Brian Anderson, one of the ten, added, "You can talk about how much you love the team, but you're in a situation where you put up or shut up. Are you a team guy?"[25]

The number one pay issue for employees is fairness. This doesn't mean you should pay everyone equally. It means people should understand how your pay system works and feel rewarded for their contributions. Moreover, remember not all rewards are financial. A great work environment is fabulously enriching to many people. You can't buy trust and appreciation, but if you build them, they'll get you outstanding talent and probably save you some money.

THE   HUDDLE

If you're a builder:

- You're more likely to enable self-organization, affinity, and loose-tight structures. Be sure to have enough structure so you can organize work and work processes, control variance, and create efficiency.

- You have more difficulty with accountability than drivers do. Set high standards, stick to them, and don't shrink from providing timely consequences—positive and negative—as appropriate.

- Stay disciplined and don't be afraid to show some strong emotions as the situation and your feelings call for them. Often, a display of genuine anger by a builder shocks employees into higher performance.

- You tend to encourage peer leaders. This is great, but take decisive action with them when they aren't performing. You tend to worry too much about their feelings.

- Use pay to distinguish rewards for performance. Paying everyone about the same sends all the wrong messages unless your performance data support it.

If you're a driver:

- You like structure but don't overdo it. Give people the autonomy they need to perform. Remember, ultimately, it's people's behaviors, not your structure, that creates high performance.

- You may be very good at execution—setting a plan and performing against it—but you tend to get too far down into the details and insist to a fault that people do things a certain way. Before you do that, make sure it's necessary. Otherwise, you won't get the ingenuity you need for innovation.

- Watch out for building too much fear into the work atmosphere. Your intense drive for results can lead people to high performance but it can also lead people to focus too much on what the negative consequences might be for failure. "Trying easier" usually gets better results.

- You may need to do a more effective job of encouraging peer leaders, especially among people who are different from you. You'll benefit by getting input and influence from a more diverse group of thinkers.

- Explain your pay decisions. Make sure people know why they're getting what they're getting and how to improve their performance and increase their rewards.

THE IMPORTANCE OF BEING ENGAGING

I started this book in early 2001, put it aside for a while to concentrate on client work, and finished the first draft in late fall. Like all Americans, and many people throughout the world, 9/11 changed my perspective. I wondered whether a book on leadership that relied on sports was very relevant; it's certainly not the most serious book you can read. Then a few things happened. I saw the torrent of layoffs after the terrorist attack and I watched people rallying around sports to raise their spirits, particularly the brilliant 2001 World Series. I realized these ideas still could be worthwhile.

In the talent shortage of 2000, companies were scrambling to become better places to work. CEOs called me every day to ask how to change their organizations. I told them my research and experience said there were several key factors in becoming a great employer. By far, the most crucial one is leadership. Engaging leaders create terrific places for people, even when the compensation, benefits, training, or workplace amenities are just OK. Then the recession came and it was business as usual at most places. It seemed like companies were fighting to get to the head of the line to see who could lay off the most people first.

Layoffs crush people and are self-defeating, especially during recession and war. What better way to slow the economy down and keep it there than to cut thousands of jobs? It's the ultimate self-fulfilling prophecy: business is off so we get rid of people who then can no longer buy our stuff leading business to fall even further. Unfortunately, by 2002, whole industries had shrunk to where they were back in 1997. Many companies had to get smaller and maybe layoffs were unavoidable in certain instances—even a few of the most enlightened leaders turned to them as a last resort.

Still, my unyielding admiration goes to those brave executives who avoid layoffs, sometimes to the point of great personal loss. These are the most engaging leaders of all. Far too many companies resort to mass firings, not only when things go bad, but when there's a hint that they won't be able to keep increasing their profits. These leaders never get it, or don't care. They think they can win without their players.

Of course, in America, the "what have you done for me lately?" economy is here to stay. It cuts both ways—for employees and companies. Even during the 2002 recession, unemployment never got close to the high levels we usually see. Leaders who laid off scores of people are going to have to change how they manage and do a lot of repair work to their reputations as businesses start to grow again. Talented people will be harder to get and keep than ever. The majority of managers don't know how to create conditions that inspire people to commit to their work and their goals. Few employees feel real loyalty. There's enormous opportunity to build workplaces where people can feel alive and joyful, learn new skills and grow, and make significant contributions to business results.

With this challenge ahead, executives need new information and proven ideas presented in new ways to help them become better leaders. Engaging leadership is vital. You engage people by adopting leadership behaviors that reconcile, or at least balance, your natural style with its opposite. I know you're not going to change your total approach; I don't want you to even try. But most of us can broaden our behaviors somewhat to be much more effective. If you can't, stop trying to lead people.

Now, at the end of 2002, as I put the finishing touches on this book, I continue to see the immense value of engaging leadership. In a tougher business environment, leaders who can't engage their followers and lead them to success are falling hard and fast. In Chicago, where I live, two of the city's most famous companies are paying the price for disengaged leadership. United Airlines, once the largest airline in the world, plunged into bankruptcy after years of management mistakes, lack of focus, poor service, and alienated workers. An employee stock ownership plan, designed to save the company, failed miserably when leaders didn't involve employee-owners in the business, even though they held the majority of the stock. Near the end, key groups of employees were so angry that they refused to make further concessions to stave off bankruptcy. At the same time, the chairman of McDonald's was forced to resign years ahead of schedule. He couldn't deliver reliable profits while leaping from strategy to strategy and avoiding tough decisions. His consensus-building style and lack of versatility prevented him from taking strong actions quickly enough, though his board and franchisees demanded them. To win in every business, leaders must engage through versatility, assemble great talent, create focus and direction, and build chemistry through trust and structure. With new, more effective leadership, these two huge organizations should survive and move forward. Their underlying assets have great

value, demand for their products is still robust, and the right leaders will get employees, customers, and shareholders smiling again.
But the greatest test of engaging leadership still lies ahead. Recently,
Dusty Baker, one of the most engaging leaders in sports, signed on
to manage the Cubs. If Baker can turn around an almost century-old
culture of losing, then we'll see the unstoppable power of engaging
leadership. Engaging your team should be easy compared to that.

HOW ENGAGING ARE YOU?

The Engaging Leader Index
© Gubman Consulting

This short inventory is designed to help you understand your leadership tendencies toward the driver or builder style and how engaging you are. Please circle the item in each pair that is most like you or most appeals to you. Some items may seem similar, but it's usually best to go with the first thing that comes to mind. Instructions for calculating your score follow this section.

1A. Answers	4A. Calm	7A. Numbers
1B. Solutions	4B. Controlled	7B. Reasons
2A. Systematic	5A. Aggressive	8A. Diligent
2B. Swift	5B. Assertive	8B. Firm
3A. Insightful	6A. Determined	9A. Relationships
3B. Decisive	6B. Tolerant	9B. Facts

10A. Future

10B. Now

11A. Restrained

11B. Easy-going

12A. Diplomatic

12B. Disciplined

13A. Talkative

13B. Responsive

14A. Competitive

14B. Obliging

15A. Efficient

15B. Adaptable

16A. Persistent

16B. Eager

17A. Adaptable

17B. Goal-driven

18A. Persuasive

18B. Humble

19A. Principles

19B. Decisions

20A. Respect

20B. Victory

21A. What

21B. Why

22A. How

22B. When

23A. Rules

23B. Freedom

24A. Investments

24B. Returns

25A. Direction

25B. Guidance

26A. Progress

26B. People

27A. Motivations

27B. Incentives

28A. Philosophical

28B. Pragmatic

29A. Planful

29B. Improvisational

30A. Learning

30B. Doing

YOUR ENGAGING LEADER SCORE

© Gubman Consulting

This score sheet will tell you how you described yourself on the Engaging Leader Index. You can see how much you prefer the driver or builder style. You also can see how engaging you are.

Circle each item that you selected on the Engaging Leader Index. Be careful because the A's and B's change columns as you move down the sheet. Next, count the number of items you circled in each column. The column with the higher score is your primary style. Subtract the lower score from the higher score. If you have a difference of ten or more between your higher score and lower score, you probably rely on that style to the exclusion of the other. If the difference between the scores is between five and nine, you can be engaging when you want to be. If the difference score is four or less, you may be quite engaging.

1A	1B
2B	2A
3B	3A
4B	4A
5A	5B
6A	6B
7A	7B
8B	8A
9B	9A
10B	10A
11A	11B
12B	12A
13A	13B
14A	14B
15A	15B
16B	16A
17B	17A
18A	18B
19B	19A
20B	20A
21A	21B
22B	22A
23A	23B
24B	24A
25A	25B
26A	26B
27B	27A
28B	28A
29A	29B
30B	30A
Driver=	Builder=

High score – Low score = How engaging you are:____

(The lower the difference, the more engaging you are.)

Chapter 1

1. David Halberstam, *Playing for Keeps* (New York: Random House, 1999), 250.

2. Paul Dickson, *Baseball's Greatest Quotations* (New York: Harper Collins, 1991), 417.

3. Halberstam, *Playing for Keeps.*

4. Douglas McGregor, *Human Side of Enterprise* (New York: McGraw-Hill, 1960).

5. "The Clock Is Ticking on the Basketball Life of Riley," *Chicago Tribune*, January 14, 2001.

6. "Vikings' Captain Survives Storms," *Chicago Tribune*, August 22, 2000.

7. "Angry Moss Says Vikings Unprepared," *The New York Times*, January 15, 2001.

8. "How Bryant and O'Neal Put Teamwork Ahead of Feuding," *The New York Times*, June 5, 2001.

9. "Mellowed Piniella Seeks Second Title," *USA Today*, October 9, 2001.

10. "Mariners Are Quick to Credit Piniella," *The New York Times*, October 8, 2000.

11. Kansas City Chiefs team page, *TheSportingNews.com*, October 9, 2001.

12. *Leadershipnow.com*, M2 Communications.

13. Center for Creative Leadership, *Leadership in Action*, Vol. 18, 1998.

14. "Manager's Food Supply Energizes the Giants," *The New York Times*, July 15, 2000.

15. Ibid.

16. "Unlikely Leader," *Chicago Tribune*, January 31, 2001.

17. Advertisement, *The New York Times*, September 16, 2001.

18. Newsroom, *Clevelandbrowns.com*, January 12, 2001.

19. "More Teachers, Fewer Screamers among NFL's Coaches," *The New York Times,* August 19, 2001.

20. Portland Trail Blazers team page, *The SportingNews.com,* October 19, 2001.

21. "Mariners Are Quick to Credit Piniella."

22. "Bulls Notes," *Chicago Tribune,* November 20, 2000.

23. "A Changed Dr. Doom Returns," *The New York Times,* September 15, 2002.

Chapter 2

1. "Playoff Payoff," *Chicago Tribune,* March 12, 2001.

2. Peter Drucker, *Management Challenges for the 21st Century* (New York: HarperBusiness, 2001).

3. Employment Policy Foundation, *The American Workplace Report 2001: Building America's Workforce for the 21st Century,* Washington, D.C., August 29, 2001.

4. Department of Labor, "A Century of Change: The U.S. Labor Force, 1950–2050" *Monthly Labor Review,* May, 2002, Vol. 125, No. 5.

5. "The 100 Best Companies to Work For," *Fortune,* February 4, 2002, Vol. 145, No. 3.

6. "Most American Workers Satisfied with Their Job," *Gallup Poll Analyses,* August 31, 2001.

7. "Effective Managers Must Evolve Their Generational Stereotypes," *Findings from the 2001 Randstad North American Employee Review,* September 2001.

8. "The Towers Perrin Talent Report," Towers Perrin, August 31, 2001.

9. "Brenly's Gambles Help Propel Arizona to NLCS," *USA Today,* October 16, 2001.

10. "The Tough Work of Turning a Team Around," *Harvard Business Review,* November-December, 2000, Vol. 78, No. 6.

Chapter 3

1. "Giants Step to the Top of the NL," *USA Today*, September 27, 2000.

2. "Good Managing Makes Player Deals Pay Off," *The New York Times*, October 22, 2000.

3. "One-Year Wonders," *Chicago Tribune*, January 18, 2001.

4. Michael Treacy and Fred Wiersema, *The Discipline of Market Leaders* (Boston: Addison-Wesley, 1992).

5. "Strong Pitching Pushes Cardinals," *USA Today*, September 13, 2000.

6. Speech to Marathon Ashland Petroleum dealers, Grosse Pointe, MI, September 11, 2000.

7. "In the Oakland A's, Some Lessons for Silicon Valley," *The New York Times*, October 1, 2000.

8. "High Roller," *ESPN, The Magazine*, April 2, 2001.

9. "The A's Front Office Makes Grade with Trades," *The Sporting News*, August 6, 2001.

10. Yankees-Mariners game report, *ESPN.com*, October 22, 2001.

11. "Yankees Know How to Play the Game off the Field, Too," *The New York Times*, November 30, 2000.

12. "Gannon Finds Home with Once-Hated Raiders," *USA Today*, December 14, 2000.

13. "49ers' Renaissance Gathers Steam," *Chicago Tribune*, October 25, 2001.

14. Ibid.

15. "Vikings Draft Tendencies: Hits on Offense, Misses on Defense," *Minneapolis StarTribune*, April 16, 2001.

16. "Black Cloud Blankets Bengals," *USA Today*, November 8, 2000.

17. "Can Jackson Get Lakers to Rebound?" *USA Today*, February 12, 2001.

18. "Iverson a Brand New Man," *USA Today*, November 22, 2000.

19. "Lakers Not Ready for Second Run at Title," *USA Today*, January 18, 2001.

20. "Ex-Bulls No Longer Producing," *Chicago Tribune*, January 24, 2001.

21. "The Golf Digest Interview: Phil Mickelson," *Golf Digest*, January, 2001, Vol. 52, No. 1.

22. "The Golf Digest Interview: Vijay Singh," *Golf Digest*, April, 2001, Vol. 52, No. 4.

23. "Basketball Notes," *Chicago Tribune*, April 4, 2001.

24. Speech to Marathon Ashland Petroleum dealers.

25. "Haslett Is Saints Keystone," *USA Today*, January 3, 2001.

26. Ibid.

27. "Perceived Lack of Communication Dooms Mueller," *ESPN.com*, May 12, 2002.

28. "The Odd Couple," *Chicago Tribune*, January 25, 2001.

29. "Ravens Talk Talk, Walk Walk," *USA Today*, January 8, 2001.

30. "From the Beginning, Pitino Was Blinded by His Ego," *The Sporting News*, January 8, 2001.

31. "Ravens Talk Talk, Walk Walk."

32. Three Bears radio show, WGN Radio 720, September 29, 2001.

33. "The Odd Couple."

34. Sign outside Michael Jordan store, United Airlines Terminal, O'Hare Field

35. "New York Capitalizes on Oakland's Mistake, Moves on to ALCS," *TheSportingNews.com*, October 16, 2001.

Chapter 4

1. Halberstam, *Playing for Keeps*, 259.

2. "The Odd Couple."

3. "Turnover at the Top," DBM, Inc., June, 2002.

4. "There's Method to Draft Savvy," *Chicago Tribune*, June 22, 2001.

5. "Shrewd Trading Has Mariners on Verge of Wins Record," *NBCSports.com*, October 5, 2001.

6. "From the Super Bowl to Super Startups," *Leaders Online*, Heidrick and Struggles, 2001.

7. Ibid.

8. "Riding the Wave: The New Global Career Culture," Career Innovation, June 1999.

9. "Chicago Clippers," *Chicago Tribune*, January 12, 2001.

10. Ibid.

11. "Work, Family Pressures Undercut Job Satisfaction," *Life Today,* National Institute of Business Management, April 2002.

12. "Breaking the Glass Ceiling: The Effects of Sex Ratios and Work-Family Human Resource Practices," Unpublished research manuscript, Prof. George F. Dreher, Indiana University, 2001.

13. "Iverson a Brand New Man."

14. Ibid.

15. "QB Bias Falls," *Chicago Tribune,* December 22, 2000.

16. "Alou Says He Hasn't Received Any Recent Offers," *ESPN.com* October 13, 2002.

17. "Agent for Marvin Lewis Accuses the Bills of Bias in Coach's Hiring," *The New York Times,* January 24, 2001.

18. "Cochran Says Black Coaches Held to Different Standard," *ESPN.com,* September 30, 2002.

19. "Best Practices in Diversity: Corporate and Candidates Perspectives," Korn Ferry, December 2001.

20. "Thrill Is Gone," *Chicago Tribune,* November 3, 2000.

21. "Piniella Won't Be Back in Seattle Next Season," *ESPN.com,* October 14, 2002.

22. "Mickelson Staying with Family after Birth of Daughter," *ESPN.com,* October 24, 2001.

23. "A Hectic Schedule Par for the Course," *Chicago Tribune,* July 16, 2000.

24. "Bruce Lietzke Watching Son Play in Abilene," *Dallas Morning News,* July 28, 1998.

25. "Family Company Relies on Employee Feedback to Shape Positive Culture," *Winningworkplaces.org.*

Chapter 5

1. "What I've Learned," *Esquire,* December, 2000, Vol. 137, No. 6.

2. "Some Things Borrowed, All Things Yankee Blue," *The New York Times,* October 29, 2000.

3. Dickson, *Baseball's Greatest Quotations,* 423.

4. Jim Collins and Jerry Porras, *Built to Last* (New York: Harper-Collins, 1997).

5. "Time for Cubs to Step Up—Or Else," *Chicago Tribune*, October 13, 2000.

6. "Hockey Notes," *Chicago Tribune*, December 26, 2000.

7. "The Ryder Cup Rumpus," *Golf Digest*, December, 1999, Vol. 50, No. 12.

8. Ibid.

9. "Bears Notes," *Chicago Tribune*, November 6, 2000.

10. "Baseball Preview 2002," *Chicago Tribune*, April 1, 2002.

11. "My Putting Musts," *Golf Magazine*, April, 2000, Vol. 42, No. 4.

12. *Sports Illustrated Tribute to Mickey Mantle*, August 21, 1995.

13. "Here's to You, Mr. Robinson," *Bergen Record*, December 19, 2000.

14. "Rams Come Up with Another Big Play in Biggest Game of the Season," *CBS.sportsline.com*, January 30, 2000.

15. "Here's to You, Mr. Robinson."

16. "From the Super Bowl to Super Startups."

17. Halberstam, *Playing for Keeps*, 281.

18. "Manuel's Plan Pans Out Just as He Envisioned," *Chicago Tribune*, September 25, 2000.

19. "High Marks in Chemistry," *Minneapolis StarTribune*, October 27, 2000.

20. Ibid.

21. "Viking Notes," *Minneapolis StarTribune*, October 25, 2001.

22. "Pitchers Put Sox in Good Position to Battle Twins," *Chicago Tribune*, June 26, 2001.

23. Dickson, *Baseball's Greatest Quotations*, 357.

24. "Fassel Foretells Playoffs for Giants," *The New York Times*, November 23, 2000.

25. Ibid.

26. "Fassel's Guarantee Has Giants on Verge of Playoffs," *The Sporting News*, December 18, 2000.

27. "Face-Lift Is in Order for NFC East Champion Giants Come Playoff Time," *CBS.sportsline.com*, December 18, 2000.

Chapter 6

1. Fastscripts at *asapsports.com*, October 9, 2000.

2. "WorkUSA 2002: Weathering the Storm," Watson Wyatt Worldwide, 2002.

3. "Giants Follow the Lead of Fassel," *The New York Times*, January 15, 2001.

4. "Dusty's Roads," *Chicago Tribune*, October 19, 2002.

5. "Baker Understands the Recipe," *Chicago Tribune*, September 9, 2000.

6. Ibid.

7. "A Mad, Mad League," *Chicago Tribune*, November 11, 2001.

8. "Versatility Gives Lowe Edge for Playoffs," *Chicago Tribune*, October 2, 2000.

9. "Wrong Ingredients Spoil 2 Seasons," *Chicago Tribune*, October 8, 2001.

10. "High Marks in Chemistry."

11. Ibid.

12. "The One," *ESPN, The Magazine* January 22, 2001.

13. Ibid.

14. "Jackson Plans to Clamp Down on Lakers," *Yahoo! Sports,* January 12, 2001.

15. "The One."

16. Ibid.

17. Ibid.

18. "Mariners Are Quick to Credit Piniella."

19. "Bowman Stands Test of Time," *Chicago Tribune*, November 8, 2000.

20. "Brown Mysteriously Absent from Practice," *USA Today*, December 19, 2000.

21. "Riley Still Living off His Magic-Laker Days," *ESPN.com*, November 7, 2001.

22. "Brenly's Gambles Help Propel Arizona to NLCS."

23. Ibid.

24. Speech to Marathon Ashland Petroleum dealers.

25. "As Leaders, Women Rule," *Business Week*, November 20, 2000.

26. *vincelombardi.com*.

27. "Ravens Talk Talk, Walk Walk."

28. "Why We Love Phil Jackson," *St. Louis Post-Dispatch*, October 3, 2001.

29. "The Celtics Are Glad Rick Pitino Has Departed and They're Showing It," *ESPN.com*, Feburary 15, 2001.

30. "Small Ego, Big Results," *MSNBCsports.com*, February 7, 2001.

31. "The Celtics Are Glad Rick Pitino Has Departed."

32. "NBA Notes," *Chicago Tribune*, March 11, 2001.

33. Halberstam, *Playing for Keeps*, 38.

34. Ibid., 41.

35. "Bulls Notes," *Chicago Tribune*, December 6, 2000.

36. "Inside the Bulls," *Chicago Tribune*, January 9, 2000.

37. "NBA Notes," *Chicago Tribune*, March 5, 2001.

38. "Inside the Bulls."

Chapter 7

1. "Sonics Fire Westphal," *Yahoo! Sports*, November 27, 2000.

2. "Repairing the Coke Machine," *Business Week*, November 19, 2001.

3. "Jauron's Message a Simple One," *Chicago Tribune*, August 25, 2000.

4. "Here's to You, Mr. Robinson."

5. Ibid.

6. "A Changed Dr. Doom Returns."

7. Ibid.

8. "Players Get 257-Page Playbook at Start of Camp," *Sportingnews .com*, October 7, 2000.

9. "Celtics Execute under O'Brien," *ESPN.com*, March 3, 2001.

10. "Arians and Fazio News Conference," *Clevelandbrowns.com*, February 5, 2001.

11. Dickson, *Baseball's Greatest Quotations*, 424.

12. "Iverson a Brand New Man."

13. "Can Jackson Get Lakers to Rebound?"

14. "Sonics Fire Westphal."

15. "With New Direction, Sonics Wallop Lakers," *USA Today,* December 1, 2000.

16. Dickson, *Baseball's Greatest Quotations,* 453.

17. "Gill Follows the Money, Stays with Nets," *Yahoo! Sports,* November 22, 2000.

18. "Baseball Report," *Chicago Tribune,* March 11, 2001.

19. Ibid.

20. "Dodgers Thrown a Curve as Sheffield Seeks Trade," *Chicago Tribune,* February 20, 2001.

21. "Waveland and Sheffield Has a Cub Ring to It," *Chicago Tribune,* March 11, 2001.

22. "Craving Star Bucks," *Chicago Tribune,* February 22, 2001.

23. "WorkUSA 2002: Weathering the Storm."

24. "Ten Diamondbacks Defer Salaries to Help Cash-Poor Team," *ESPN.com,* February 20, 2001.

25. Ibid.

Bulk Pricing Information

For special discounts on
20 or more copies of
The Engaging Leader
call Dearborn Trade Special Sales
at 800-621-9621, ext. 4410
or e-mail rowland@dearborn.com.
You'll receive great service
and top discounts.

For added visibility, please
consider our custom cover service,
which highlights your firm's name
and logo on the cover.
We are also an excellent resource
for dynamic and
knowledgable speakers.